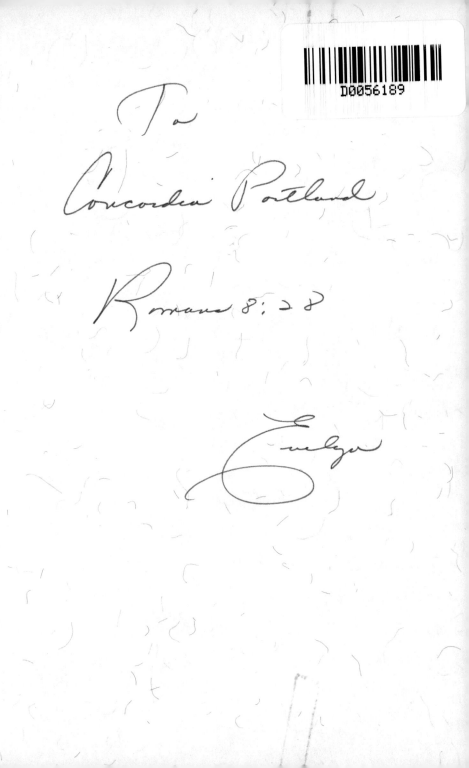

To

Concordia Portland

Romans 8:28

Evelyn

GAINING THROUGH LOSING

Evelyn Christenson

assisted editorially by Viola Blake

VICTOR BOOKS

a division of SP Publications, Inc.
WHEATON. ILLINOIS 60187

Offices also in Fullerton, California • Whitby, Ontario, Canada • Amersham-on-the-Hill, Bucks, England

Other books by Evelyn Christenson:
What Happens When Women Pray
"Lord, Change Me!"
Two by Evelyn

EVELYN CHRISTENSON is chairman of the board of
United Prayer Ministries, Minneapolis, Minnesota and
speaks frequently at retreats, conventions, and seminars
on the subject of prayer. Cassette tapes from a *"Lord,
Change Me!"* seminar are available for $22.95. Also availa-
ble are cassette tapes of an Evelyn Christenson prayer
seminar based on her book, *What Happens When Women
Pray* at $20.95. Write Evelyn Christenson, 4265 Brigadoon
Drive, St. Paul, MN 55112.

Most of the Scripture quotations in this book are from the King
James Version. Other quotations are from the New International
Version (NIV), © 1978 by The New York International Bible So-
ciety; the New American Standard Bible (NASB), © 1960, 1962,
1963, 1968, 1971, 1973 by the Lockman Foundation, La Habra,
California; the Revised Standard Version (RSV), © 1946 and
1952, the Division of Christian Education, National Council of
Churches of Christ in the U.S.A.; the New Scofield Reference
Bible (SCO), © 1967 by Oxford University Press; and the New
English Bible (NEB), © 1961 by Oxford University Press and the
Syndics of the Cambridge University Press.

Recommended Dewey Decimal Classification: 248.4
   Suggested Subject Headings: CHRISTIAN LIFE, SPIRITUAL LIFE, FAITH

Library of Congress Catalog Card Number: 80-51630
ISBN: 0-8B207-795-3

VICTOR BOOKS
A division of SP Publications, Inc.
P. O. Box 1825 • Wheaton, Illinois, 60187

Table of Contents

Dedication

To my dear ones who prayed fervently and unceasingly for fourteen months while I was writing this book, praying God's will for each thought and every word:

My prayer chains who not only communicated my every physical, emotional, mental, and spiritual need, but fervently and faithfully prayed—

Mother and Rollie who prayed daily whether or not they knew my specific needs—

Mother Chris who spent so many of her hours in her rocking chair praying for me—

Chris who understood and undergirded me in prayer when the hours were too long and the task too great—

All those other dear family members and friends who sensed needs and prayed so often—

To them—my indescribable thanks.

To God—all the glory.

Discovery

Introduction

I have discovered through the years a most astounding principle at work in my life: gains actually come through the seeming-losses.

When I was just 23 years of age, I took as my philosophy of life the promise in Romans 8:28—that God was working out all things for my good because I love Him. But *how* He was doing it has slowly unraveled before my eyes year after year. God has not removed every loss, hurt, or difficulty. But He has worked *through* them—turning each of them into a gain.

Every one of my *gaining-through-losing* experiences is backed by a biblical precept. And God has put the two together—my experiences and His teaching—until my losses due to circumstances and this world's natural course of events have produced a life of gains. I have sometimes failed to do my part, but even so God has *always* worked out every loss for my gain—when I let Him.

But I have two regrets in writing this book. The first is that there was not enough space to include the myriad of other gains through losses—some small and others large—which came into focus as I reviewed and analyzed my life in the writing of this manuscript.

The second regret is that some of the most profound gains have come through losses which cannot be recorded in a book. There are those heartbreaking experiences which I've worked through with family and friends that are much too private to share. Those times when together we've discovered God's amazing gains as He counseled, comforted, and healed us.

Then there are those deep times of my life that forever will be only between my God and myself. Wounds and losses that are not for human eyes nor human understanding. Those times when God has walked so closely by my side, sometimes explaining the whys and other times just silently assuring me of His presence.

And then there must be an eternity full of surprises. Those millions of gains-through-losses which I never even knew happened here on earth. Waiting to be unveiled to my astounded mind—in heaven.

But here *is* a whole book full of fabulous gains I've already discovered and which I *can* share. Share in the hope that they will help you discover in your everyday hurts or calamitous tragedies that God is also standing by—ready and anxious to turn your losses into gains.

1

Gaining Through God's "So Thats"

Do you always win? Or do you sometimes lose? If you do, God is in the business of turning your losses into gains.

It was back in 1965, as I lay fretting in my hospital bed recovering from gallbladder surgery, that God began to teach me the gaining through losing principle. Here I was struggling against having to be in that bed because I was missing all the exciting things He was doing in our church those days. As I reached for my pillow radio receiver, I searched the local stations until I heard a familiar voice. It was that of a pastor friend chatting to us "shut-ins" between musical numbers and poetry reading. Suddenly I heard him say, "The title of this poem is 'Gaining Through Losing.'"

And I was about to discover one of the greatest of all discoveries about God—as he read:

I asked God for strength, that I might achieve,
   I was made weak, that I might learn humbly to obey,
I asked for health, that I might do greater things,
   I was given infirmity, that I might do better
     things.
I asked for riches, that I might be happy,

I was given poverty, that I might be wise.
I asked for power, that I might have the praise
    of men,
    I was given weakness, that I might feel the need
    of God.
I asked for all things, that I might enjoy life,
    I was given life, that I might enjoy all things.
I got nothing that I asked for—but everything I had
    hoped for.
    Almost despite myself, my unspoken prayers were
    answered.
I am, among all men, most richly blessed.
    Suddenly I came alive. I had discovered God's "so that"
principle!

As I've studied the Bible, I have discovered that every facet in God's dealing with His people—with you and me—seems to include a "so that." In effect God says to us, "I am permitting this unpleasant experience *so that* you may *gain* . . . *so that* you may *gain* a new insight, *so that* you will be *richer* in your experiences and thereby help someone going through a similar problem." Nothing with God is haphazard, coincidental, or happenstance. Problems in our lives do not mean that God has lost control or that He is no longer on His throne, but they give us the glorious opportunity to prove God's "so thats"—*so that* we might gain through our losses.

That anonymous poem, believed to have been found on the body of a Civil War soldier, had jolted me—yes, shaken me out of my self-pity. Could it be true? Could God take what seems to be a loss and through it give me something better? Could He turn bitter losses into fabulous gains?

From that day to this, I have been discovering God's "so thats" throughout the Bible and His applications of them in my personal life. Through the years God has unfolded some of the magnitude of this principle to me. When we let Him, He takes our losses and shows us His great "so thats"—so that we can have or be more than before. He works our losses all out for our gains. That day, I thought the poem applied to the giving of my body to the Lord, but that was only the immediate result. Today, I can fill this whole book with God's "so thats"—how He takes our *losses* and turns them into *gains*.

What do those two little words *so that* really mean? *The Random House Dictionary of the English Language* (p. 1350) gives these definitions for *so that*: "in order that," "with the effect or result." It involves the reasons, the whys of life. Even the little word *that* is defined as "expressing cause or reason, purpose or aim, result or consequence" (p. 1470).

The Bible is full of God's "so thats." Paul tells us that the things which happened to him had "fallen out rather unto the furtherance of the gospel; *so that* my bonds in Christ are manifest in all the palace and in all other places" (Phil. 1:12-13). He also explains a "so that" to the members of the church of the Thessalonians: "You became followers of us, and of the Lord, having received the word in much affliction, with joy of the Holy Ghost; *so that* you were examples to all that believe" (1 Thes. 1:6-7). Then Jesus, before restoring sight to the man blind from birth, must have startled His disciples with His answer to their question, "Who did sin, this man, or his parents?" He replied, "Neither has this man sinned, nor his parents; but *that* the works of God should be made manifest in him" (John 9:3).

Jesus' "So That" Principle

Jesus both taught and lived this "so that" principle. He repeatedly explained it in the seeming paradox of "gaining through losing." He summed it up in His words, "Whosoever will lose his life for My sake shall find it" (Matt. 16:26). Lose life *so that* you can gain it? Yes, Jesus said you must lose your life *so that* you can find it. It will be *through* your loss that you can actually gain. Then Jesus used the

most valuable possession we have to teach this lesson—
our lives.

For whosoever will save his life shall lose it: and
whosoever will lose his life for My sake shall find
it (Matt. 16:25).

How unpopular that philosophy must have been in His
day! And how unpopular it is today. Somehow people
can't handle losing. We don't think of losing as something
that can be positive. We are a success-oriented society.
Losing is unpleasant. Losing is failure, and failure is
doom. We are taught how to win, but we have little or no
teaching on how to lose.

Can losing life actually produce gain and the finding of
life? From our rat-race perspective, it seems that Jesus had
things a little mixed-up. Was He not facing the reality of
the hard, cold facts? Didn't He understand the sting, pain,
and sorrow of losing—especially losing what we call *life*?
"Whosoever *loses* his life for My sake shall *find* it"?

What is Life?

But what is life—that elusive something we humans are
chasing, seeking, and so frantically pursuing? Is it utopia,
a never-never land of euphoric happiness? Is it what we
Christians are seeking to have "more abundantly"? Intan-
gible, indescribable, yet we believe we will recognize it
when we find it.

We seek *life* in health spas for the body beautiful, in
doctors' offices for vigorous health, in a regimented lifestyle for longevity. We look for it in ever-changing sports
fads, in shorter workweeks, in hobbies to take the bore-
dom out of our leisure time. We hoard money in banks to
ensure a life of comfort. We invest in stocks and insurance
for security at retirement, or in property to achieve equity.
We search for life through education, equal rights, mind-
expanding programs, and through the passive search for
tranquility. We strive for it by moving up to the right
neighborhood, being involved socially, getting to the top

professionally, by being needed. We know we will reach it when we are free from an addiction or a habit or a confinement. And we will clinch it all by marrying the love of our life and moving into our dream house. Then there will be life—lived "happily ever after"!

But somehow, no matter how many of these we find, there is always the haunting feeling that there must be more to life than this. One of the highest incidences of suicide today is among the affluent, popular so-called "beautiful people"—those who have attained most of these.

Well, then, perhaps life after all is just the seeking of it —that life is found in the process of seeking it. Is it true that the pursuit of it, to which we are all constitutionally entitled, brings happiness? Or can we really find it?

Then, if we can find life, will we really find it through Jesus' mind-jarring paradox of "gaining it through losing it"? I decided to find out.

A word of caution here: This principle has nothing to do with a martyr complex or suicidal tendencies. Jesus never leads us to commit suicide. Nor does this principle have to do with the masochistic tendency to seek gratification from pain, deprivation, or self-denial. It does not apply to those who enjoy losing, but to those plain, ordinary, everyday followers of Christ who are *willing* to lose their lives—for His sake.

One evening, while looking up the biblical definition of that word *lose* for this book, I was shocked at the synonyms: "kill, annihilate, put an end to." Turning to my husband I said, "Chris, I can't write something I can't live. How do I really lose, put an end to, my life for Christ's sake?"

"Well, I think you have already accomplished 99 percent of it," he reassured me.

"Then this must be a huge 1 percent with which I'm struggling," I sighed.

The next Sunday was Easter. Before dawn I spent three

hours in deep prayer, begging God to show me what it meant to lose my life. Agonizing prayer—punctuated with hot tears. Then gradually, the answer seemed to come from God: "Empty yourself of all of you, Evelyn."

I thought I had done this many times before. I had certainly tried to through years of serving Him. But God showed me there was still more of self to be relinquished. Looking back, I see that there always had been more. After I would pray, "Nothing of me, Lord," sooner or later He would show me another area of my life to lose. And so that Easter morning, I struggled hard to discover the "all of me." I was confident that God had just given the answer, but somehow the whole sense of "losing" was not there yet. I still strained to find it.

The next morning my secretary came to work with a puzzled look on her face. Then she said, "I was really struggling in prayer early yesterday morning. But it wasn't for me. I kept saying, 'But this is Easter, Lord. I should be rejoicing, but I'm not!' Ev, it was somebody else I was praying for, but I don't know who." Then I told her how I too was struggling during those very same hours. She looked up at me in amazement and exclaimed, "Oh, it was *you*!"

Then I decided to try an experiment. I can handle things in little slots of time better than attempting something forever and ever. So the next Friday I said, "Lord, this weekend I want to lose my whole life completely for Jesus' sake as I go to Canada to bring this prayer seminar." Then, at the Holiday Inn in Ottawa before starting to teach on Saturday morning, I spent more than an hour in sincere, expectant prayer. "Father, today is the day. Empty me of all of me."

I had prayed that prayer a thousand times before, but this time it was different—deeper, more desperate. "Take *all* of me. Every deep, hidden, unspoken, unrecognized desire for acclaim. Please, no *desire* to have anybody talk about how my books are selling; no *desire* for praise or statistics; no *desire* for people's gratitude for the ministry; no *desire* for Evelyn even to be seen or her voice heard. Take it all out, Lord—*all*."

As my prayertime drew to a close, there was an unexpected shift in the direction of my prayers. Something was *coming* instead of *leaving*. It was a surprise because I really wasn't expecting the answer to be something I could feel. I'd only had vague thoughts about somehow nothing of me in the seminar that day. But suddenly I felt pouring into my very being a sensation I had not known before. A brand-new emotion I'd never experienced in 48 years of walking with God. Something warm and radiant, soft yet bright, swelling inside me until it engulfed me. I stayed motionless on my knees, hardly daring to breathe lest I disturb that new something. What was it? Life? The kind of life Jesus promised when we lose ours for His sake?

A couple of hours later, I sought to explain my new exuberant attitude in the opening remarks at the seminar, but words failed. I tried *joy*. No. I've had joy from God before, lots of joy. *Fulfillment?* No. After a great expression of family love or a deep moving of God in a seminar, I've often said, 'If I get any more fulfilled, I'll explode." But there it was. The *life* Jesus gives—that came when I wanted to lose mine for His sake. When I wanted to give all of me for Him. Abounding, exuberant, unspeakable life!

A week later I received in the mail a poem entitled "Treasures," by Martha Snell Nicholson. How well it expresses what God had taught me.

> One by one He took them from me.
>   All the things I valued most
> Until I was empty-handed;
>   Every glittering toy was lost.

> And I walked earth's highways,
>   grieving,
>   In my rags of poverty.

> Till I heard His voice inviting
>   "Lift your *empty* hands to Me!"
>   (italics mine)
>
> So I held my hands toward heaven,
>   And He filled them with a store
> Of His own transcendent riches
>   Till my hands could hold no more.
>
> And at last I comprehended
>   With my stupid mind and dull
> That God could not pour His riches
>   Into hands already full.
>   (*Her Best for the Master*, comp.
>   F. J. Wiens, Moody Press)

We frantically scurry around looking for life in all the things we have and do, when all along the secret is in the *losing*. We can't be filled with two things at one time; so it is a matter of being emptied—emptied *so that* Christ can fill us—with His life.

I'm sure there will always be more. More of Him when there is less of me. But for now I'm also sure I have discovered the secret, the formula for finding and gaining life—radiant, abundant life. *Losing* it for Jesus' sake.

Losing my life *so that* I can find it.

Jesus' "So That" Formula

Let's look at Jesus' "so that" formula for finding life in its scriptural setting. (See Matt. 16:13-27.) His teaching, "Whosoever will lose his life for My sake shall find it," was given to His disciples right after His command: "Follow Me." Follow Him? Where? How?

In the preceding incident, Jesus had just told them that His own "so that" would be *losing* His life through suffering and dying *so that* the *gaining* could come in resurrection on the third day. From Peter's reaction in rebuking

Christ, it seems that he heard only the losing. He apparently missed Christ's intended *so that*—His absolute, once-for-all victory over sin and death on that cross. Peter missed Christ's triumphant rising which gave assurance to all future Christians (see 1 Cor. 15). He missed the fact that the cross was not the end, but just the "so that" of unleashing the redeeming power that was to surge throughout all of Planet Earth.

In fact, Peter decided to nip the whole process in the bud. He probably was feeling a little puffed up. Hadn't Jesus told Peter that his declaration that He was "the Christ, the Son of the living God" had come to him from the Father in heaven? So Peter, thinking he knew God's ways even better than Christ, rebuked Him with an "I won't let this happen to You" attitude (Matt. 16:22).

How often I have played Peter and looked at others, deciding that their seeming-losses could not possibly be God's will for them! It has taken years for me to begin to recognize God's perfect "so that" plan for those I love or counsel. I too prefer to protect them from God's frequent way of giving gains through losses.

It is frightening to see that Jesus' answer involved calling Peter "Satan." His words must have stung: "Get thee behind Me, Satan. Thou art an offense unto Me; for thou savourest not the things that are of God, but those that be of men," (v. 23). How could Peter have come so far from knowing God's way since God had just revealed such great divine information to him?

Satan, that supernatural being, the Adversary who *always* opposes God's will, was, of course, especially against the event that would bring his own ultimate and utter defeat—the Cross. It was frightening too since two members of the Godhead, the Father and the Son, definitely were ascribing to this "gaining through losing" process. I wonder how many of Satan's seeming-gains he substitutes for God's process of gaining through losing. Temporary gains, which he knows all along will be our ultimate loss. Satan's plan is always for our eventual and then eternal loss.

I wonder too how many times Jesus ascribes my misunderstanding of God's way for myself and others to Satan's desire for me to miss God's will. How much *life* have I kept others from experiencing because I could not see God's "gaining through losing" process, His "so that"? How does Jesus view my thoughts when I think God could not possibly want me to lose something for Jesus' sake? How many of His "so thats" have I missed?

But that "Follow Me" was the last of Jesus' three-part formula for finding life.

> Then said Jesus unto His disciples, "If any man will come after Me, let him deny himself, and take up his cross, and follow Me" (Matt. 16:24).

If anybody will come after Me, triumph with Me, experience the victory I am going to experience—here is the formula:

First, *deny yourself.* That was what I was trying to learn to do Easter week. But what is myself? Is it my personal ambitions, my aspirations, my self-seekings, my self-assertions—doing what I like to do? Must I voluntarily abandon all these? Must I always say *No* to me?

After I had struggled in prayer on that Easter morning, I sat alone reading through John's account of Christ's resurrection and the events which followed. I stopped abruptly when I came to "Peter . . . lovest thou Me more than these?" (John 21:15) Peter, with the other disciples, had gone back to his former occupation—fishing. When he recognized Jesus on the shore preparing breakfast, Peter, having denied not himself but Jesus on the way to the cross, jumped into the water in his eagerness to reach Christ. When breakfast was finished, Jesus turned to Peter and asked that piercing question, "Lovest thou Me more than these?"

I pondered the "more than these" for a long time. *More than what? All the things Peter had gone back to even after knowing Jesus was no longer dead? Back to fishing, the challenge of the sea, the wind in his face, the familiar roll of the boat? An occupation, a miraculous catch of fish?* I wondered too what *my* "more than these" might be. The boat spray in *my* face, *my* house, *my* loved ones?

That afternoon at our family Easter dinner, I was still thinking about my "more than these." I looked at my children whom I love so deeply. My heart was aching as I silently prayed, "How could I stop loving *them*, Lord? Lose them for Your sake? My own flesh and blood?" Then suddenly, as if He were seated at the table with us, He clearly said, *"More*—don't love them more than you love Me." And then I knew that for me, "these things" were anything I put ahead of Him—my priorities.

In our prayer seminars when we are giving the most important thing in our lives (material possessions, a human relationship, or a circumstance) to God for His will, many are hesitant to pray that prayer, fearing that God will automatically take away all they give Him. But that is not usually the case. God only wants us to be willing to give up all for Him, to love Him more than we love all these other things.

I have found that when I really learn to do this, the process of gaining through losing starts in my life. Then, and only then, do I begin to find *life* as Jesus intended it to be for me. Then I begin to understand the marvel of His "so that."

The second part of Jesus' formula for finding life is not getting rid of something, but *taking up* something—my cross. The disciples knew well what taking up a cross meant. Many times they had seen the condemned ones compelled to carry the instruments on which they would be killed. Did Jesus mean that we were to take up the life for which the cross stood—a life of sacrifice? Did He mean that even when our cross would be bearing a trial that points to even a worse one to come? Are we still to pick it up willingly?

God explained to me a little of His secret of gaining life through the losing process of the cross at Arrowhead Springs. In the fall of 1970 in the wee hours of the night, I was praying about living the victorious Christian life. Suddenly, the chiming of bells filled the still night air with "Jesus, lover of my soul, let me to Thy bosom fly." I arose and stood on the porch in silence, spellbound as the full moon glistened on the softly rustling palm fronds. But my eyes looked heavenward, pleading with God. "I can't live this life," I prayed. "I can't do it."

"No," came the answer, "but Christ can live it in you." Then, as I waited for more, God brought Galatians 2:20 to my mind. The mystery of that verse began to unravel before me.

> I am *crucified* with Christ. Nevertheless I *live*. Yet not I, but *Christ lives in me*. (Here and in all succeeding biblical references, the italics are mine.)

Not just *into* a cross experience, but *through* a cross experience—into life. Jesus living His life in me—resurrected, victorious *life!*

Yes, point three of Jesus' formula is "Follow Me." Did Jesus look at Peter when He said that? Was He telling Peter and all the rest of us to get behind Him and follow Him, not try to lead Him? "You do the following, I'll do the leading." I almost can hear Jesus saying, "Follow Me—even though it is going to involve denial, sacrifice, and losing yourself. Whosoever will save his life shall lose it, and whosoever will lose his life for My sake shall find it."

So the losses of life don't need to stop at being losses. In God's hands they can be *so that* we can gain life—real life—not only for eternity, but also for right here, today.

Losing my self-seeking *so that* I can *gain* Christ's fulfilling, joyous, abundant life? That's quite a bargain!

"O God, help me, *lose* my life *so that* I can *gain* Christ's in me."

2

Paul's Gaining Through Losing

Paul's writings seem to exude, almost overflow, with this gaining-through-losing philosophy of Jesus. Was his victorious, abundant life the result of having actually lived Jesus' teaching that we find life through losing it? Yes, Paul himself sums up his attitude toward life in his letter to the Philippians:

> But what things were *gain* to me, those I counted *loss* for Christ (Phil. 3:7).

God has used one of Paul's "gaining through losing" experiences in my life through the years. It is recorded in 2 Corinthians 12:7-10:

> And lest I should be exalted above measure through the abundance of the revelations, there was given to me a thorn in the flesh, the messenger of Satan to buffet me, lest I should be exalted above measure. For this thing I besought the Lord thrice, that it might depart from me. And He said unto me, "My grace is sufficient for thee; for My strength is made perfect in weakness." Most gladly therefore will I rather glory in my infirmities, that the power of Christ may rest

19

upon me. Therefore I take pleasure in infirmities, in reproaches in necessities, in persecutions, in distresses for Christ's sake; for when I am weak, then am I strong.

Since I was 18, I have underlined, dated, and made notes beside these verses in all the Bibles I have owned. They are Paul's account of what he *gained* at the time he *lost*, received a "no" answer from the Lord. He reveals what he gained *through* a seeming-loss when he prayed three times for his thorn in the flesh to be removed.

I too have prayed about a disfiguring, annoying, hindering thorn in my flesh. For more than 10 years, one or both of my eyes occasionally swell almost shut. Although God has spoken to me through this portion of Scripture many times, He brought it into focus in May of 1965 when I prayed, as Paul did, that He would remove my thorn.

Power of Christ

I was scheduled to bring a prayer seminar to Agape Atlanta, the pilot project of the international Here's Life undertaking. Six hundred Christians were to gather the next day to learn the power of prayer for this endeavor. Since it was one of my early attempts to teach all the precepts of my book, *What Happens When Women Pray* (Victor) in one day, I had planned carefully. I had timed and recorded the points which could be included on each subject, sifted to find material which best illustrated these points, and then separated each subject into individual file folders to keep the five-to-six hours of lecturing and prayer exercises organized.

Just before going to sleep on the night before the seminar, I was reading 2 Corinthians 12. When I came to the end of verse 9, "that the power of Christ may rest upon me," I closed my Bible, held it close, and prayed a simple prayer: "Lord, tomorrow I want the power of Christ, only the power of Christ." Then I went to sleep with that prayer on my lips and on my heart.

The next morning I awoke aghast. My eyes were swelling! I knew that if the swelling continued, I would not be able to read any of my so carefully prepared notes! Envisioning the potential confusion, I panicked and started praying desperately that God would take care of the problem. Then He gently asked me a question: "What did you pray last night?"

"Oh," I said almost aloud as I remembered—"I want the power of Christ tomorrow." Then a new kind of prayer emerged: "Lord, if You are going to show me the power of Christ by my inability to refer to my notes all day, OK. I'm willing to speak to 600 people and trust You to tell me what to say." The swelling stopped at the point of my barely being able to see. I relaxed, and went to that seminar without the ability to glance at my notes—but with a tremendous sense of the power of Christ resting in me.

Studying that word *rest* as used by Paul in 2 Corinthians 12:9, I found it meant "pitching a tent over me, taking up dwelling in me." In the margin of my Bible near that word, I had written, with the Atlanta date, "I could *feel* it!" For the first time I too had experienced what it was like to have the power of Christ resting on me. Not that I hadn't experienced His power before, but this was so tangible. Speaking for five hours with more strength at the end than when I started!

I also found this process which I discovered that day was not a once-for-all experience. I am frequently astounded at the way I gain momentum as I teach and share at seminars hour after hour without a break. My normal human power during a long day unwinds like a clock running slower and slower until it stops. But not Christ's power. His limitless, divine omnipotence actually takes up residence in me. What a gain for a seeming-loss!

Apparently Paul was not asking for a "so that," but it was what the Lord gave him. I certainly wasn't praying for a "so that" either. Paul most likely prayed fervently, expectantly, for a "yes" answer, but the Lord taught him that there are times when He answers "NO"—*so that* He can give something better than what was prayed for. Gaining through losing!

God's "No" Answer

As far as we know, the Lord's "no" answer to Paul stood for the rest of his life. God did not remove his thorn in the flesh. In verse 10 Paul identifies his thorn as an *infirmity* (sometimes translated "weakness"). Vine's *Expository Dictionary of New Testament Words* (Revell, p. 204) defines this word as "want of strength, inability to produce results." This word in the Greek always means a physical weakness.

This same word *infirmity* was used by Luke the physician to describe a woman Jesus saw. For 18 years, she was "bowed together" (indicating a curvature) with a "spirit of infirmity," and could not straighten up. Even the source of her problem, Satan, was the same as Paul's. But when Jesus laid His hands on her, "immediately she was made straight and glorified God" (See Luke 13:11-17).

It is interesting that Paul had addressed these three prayers, not to the Father, but to the Lord—to Jesus. I questioned in my heart why this same Jesus took opposite action with those two whose problems were identified by the same Greek word. Also did one of them glorify God more than the other? Evidently not, according to the Scripture. The woman glorified God in her healing. Paul glorified Him in his continuing infirmity.

That opposite dealing by Jesus with similar results took place in a recent prayer seminar in California. Just before the prayertime when we give every facet of our lives, including our bodies, to God for His will, I was preparing the participants for His possible answers. I told of times when God had gloriously healed. Then I told about Elmy, my friend, for whom we had prayed much. God did not make her well. But He used her continuing infirmity, which kept her at home, to enable her to be the chairman of our Rockford telephone prayer chains and to become one of the most powerful intercessors I know.

We broke for lunch after audibly and individually, in our groups of four, giving all of ourselves to God for His will. As the session closed, two women with similar "infirmities" came to the platform to talk with me. The first, a former missionary, came bounding up the several steps, exclaiming, "Look at me, look at me. I walked up those stairs!" Noting my puzzled expression, she beamed triumphantly and went on: "Because of a knee problem and surgery, I haven't walked up steps for four years. I also have a heart condition, and I get severe headaches because of the osteoarthritis in my neck." Later she wrote a letter assuring me that the pain and inability to walk, which disappeared the moment she gave them to God, still had not recurred.

Then the other woman, her neck in a thick brace, laboriously made her way up the steps. "I prayed the same prayer too." And she beamed just as triumphantly. "But God did not choose to heal me just now." She told me of her former deep involvement in serving God, but then she was struck with a disability which stopped it all. Lowering her head and her voice, she added with a smile, "I am one of your Elmys. I have been called to pray. I sleep in traction every night and spend hours praying, and I now have time to pray during the day. God has shown me the magnitude of the job to which He has called me." Which one had the better answer from Jesus? The greater gain?

Sometimes we can experience *losing* through *gaining* when there is a "yes" answer. The psalmist tells us that "He gave them their requests, but sent leanness into their soul" (Ps. 106:15).

In her magazine, *The Hiding Place*, Corrie ten Boom says it like this:

> I see certain things that I asked for which were
> not granted. In recalling each individual circum-

stance, I am grateful now that God did not give me what I asked for. This shows that we should always pray with an attitude of reverent submission to the overruling wisdom and love of our heavenly Father.

Had God responded "Yes" to my desperate prayer to keep my eyes from swelling, what leanness of soul might I have had? I would have missed the great experience of sensing the identifiable, overwhelming feeling of the power of Christ on me all through that strenuous day! What a loss would have been mine! And how about Paul? How could God give him *gain* through a "No" answer to his petition for the removal of his infirmity?

Lessons from the "No" Answer

Paul explained that the Lord told him how this would be turned into gain. He was teaching Paul two of life's greatest lessons. Lessons that apply in turn to all those who can call Jesus "Lord," those who have a living personal relationship with Him.

The first lesson Jesus taught Paul was, *"My grace is sufficient for you"* (see 2 Cor. 12:9). As long as he had this infirmity (evidently up to the time of his death), there would be grace enough to cover all the difficulties brought on by it. How Paul would need that lesson, not only in his infirmity, but also in the trials, tribulations, imprisonments, shipwrecks, and eventual martyrdom that were to come!

Then in His answer, the Lord taught Paul another powerful lesson. *"My strength is made perfect in weakness"* (v. 9). (Paul repeated this thought in verse 10 by concluding with, "for when I am weak, then am I strong.") It is not physical strength that counts, but the power of Christ which takes up its abode, and pitches its tent over our bodies when we are weak. What was Paul's (or my) maximum strength compared with Christ's omnipotence? In comparison to Christ's infinite, limitless power, all the strength we could ever muster, rolled into one gigantic push, would pale like a firefly competing with a nuclear explosion. What did Paul gain when the Lord said "No" to his being at his best physically? What do I gain? The *strength* of the omnipotent Christ!

Listening to my husband preach over the years, I have become acutely aware of the unusual, powerful strength of his messages when his body has not been at its best. Somehow when there has been no way Chris could deliver a sermon in his own strength, that was the time the Lord stepped in and poured out His power through Chris. No "bootstrap Christianity" this.

If you are losing what you think is best for you by getting an apparent "no" answer from the Lord, take heart. It was *because* Paul's thorn in the flesh remained that the Lord could show him His mysterious dealings with His own—how He equips us through our seeming-losses. How much more powerful, effective, and fruitful Paul was because of that "no" answer! Enough grace and enough power!

Lest Pride

The dates and notes in the margins of my Bibles marched on. There was a progression of events in my learning through my swollen eyes. Atlanta was only the beginning of my being taught from 2 Corinthians 12. That same May held more lessons.

The swelling of my eyes is not particularly painful, but it is definitely disfiguring. The last Sunday of that month I was to teach a large Sunday School class and, for personal reasons, I felt I had to be at my best. Again I woke with my eyes swelling. But this time the answer came first. God simply said to me, "Exalted above measure" (v. 7).

Again I prayed—this time not that God would keep them from swelling—but only that He would *cleanse the sin of pride*. Then I asked Him to bring other sins of pride to my mind, one at a time. And He did. The events of the previous week marched before me in an ugly parade. On

Monday the religion editor of our largest local newspaper had featured the leading Christian influences in our area, my ministry being among them. I found myself basking in comments from all directions. Tuesday I was puffed up from congratulations given at a faculty appreciation dinner. Saturday noon found me smugly acknowledging recognition at a college alumni luncheon. That same night a speck of haughtiness welled up within as I brought greetings from faculty members of a great seminary with whom I had been teaching an extension course.

Horrified at what He paraded before my mind, I begged God to forgive all those awful attitudes. Then I prayed that He would cleanse me of them all.

I had recorded in my notes: "Suddenly I felt one of those rare experiences—could *feel* the power (of Christ) come into my body. Very real!" I had learned a little four-lettered reason for my thorn in the flesh—*lest* pride.

Paul obviously struggled with pride too, for he used this word *lest* to introduce the reason for his thorn in the flesh:

> Lest any man should think of me above that which he sees me to be, or that he heareth of me.
> And lest I should be exalted above measure . . . there was given to me a thorn in the flesh (2 Cor. 12:6-7).

Random House Dictionary (p. 822) defines *lest* as: "The *so that* used negatively to introduce . . . an occurrence requiring caution." "For fear that"—God's yellow caution flag. Watch out!

Paul said *so that* I won't be exalted above measure by others or myself, God allowed a deterrent—lest.

The other day another author and I were discussing how pride makes me a loser. "When Satan can't get at me in defeat," I told her, "he gets me in my successes—with pride."

Then she asked, "How do you handle standing ovations, announcements of booksellers' ratings, and so forth?"

"I constantly keep in mind that God spells pride just one way, *s-i-n*," I explained. "And when there is sin in my life, I know from years of experience that God does not come in power in my ministry. That knowledge becomes the greatest deterrent to sinning that there is in my life. I don't *dare* give pride a place."

Some authorities have suggested that Paul's "infirmity" most likely was disfiguring. We don't really know. But whatever it was, it kept him from being proud. It was used by God as a deterrent in his life too.

Who of us has not had some physically disfiguring thorn? Not many of us feel that there is no need for improvement. Too fat/skinny, too short/tall, noses too big/small. Then, how many of us have something that is *really* disfiguring? Are we as willing to learn as much from our thorns as Paul was willing to learn from his? Can we really say we have *gained* as much as Paul gained by a "no" answer, a *loss*?

An infirmity is not only a deterrent to the sin of pride. How much nicer Paul must have been to know, to be close to, when there was a *loss* in his life. We too tend to be slightly arrogant, unreachable, overly self-confident when everything is a *gain* for us.

It took me a long time to face the fact that perhaps the *why* of my swelling eyes was a deterrent—to the sin of pride. Had it been an answer to my mother's daily prayer, "God, don't let Evelyn get proud?" Could God's "way of escape" (1 Cor. 10:13) from the temptation of pride possibly be a disfigurement?

More Lessons?

But there was more instruction for me from 2 Corinthians 12. The following September I flew to British Columbia after finishing speaking at a three-day retreat on Mount Rainier the afternoon before.

I awoke exhausted, shattered, and unnerved the next morning—facing an all-day seminar, a dinner meeting, and then a rally that night. I didn't know how I could get through that day. And there it was again—a badly swollen eye. The notes I jotted down that morning are interesting now: "None of the other lessons from this Scripture fit." So I prayed, "God, teach me the lesson You have for me." "Suddenly," continued my notes, "I could *thank* Him for this eye, asking, pleading for Him to be *glorified* through it."

Then Philippians 4:13 flashed into my mind: "I can do all things through Christ who strengthens me." "'*All things*'—even this schedule," I wrote. As I turned to read it in my Bible, I was struck by the preceding verse, ". . . I am *instructed* both to be full and to be hungry, both to abound and to suffer need" (v. 12). I turned over on my back, looked up to God, and started to pray Ephesians 3:20: "Now unto Him that is able to do exceeding abundantly above all that we ask or think . . ." Tears popped into my eyes—HIM! CHRIST! The power of Christ of 2 Corinthians 12! Jesus!

I concluded my notes with, "A few minutes later the eye is draining already. Usually day or two later. Instructed *enough*? That's what I'm feeling.'

The lessons are progressing. Just before a large seminar in California this spring, my eyes started to swell. But my only reaction was to smile up at God and relax in Him. I'm learning His will!

"Thanks, God, I Needed That!"

As I write this chapter, I'm at a booksellers' national convention. Have I learned the last lesson? Evidently not.

My assignment yesterday was to speak about the power of books—my books. In the middle of the night I agonized in prayer over what I said. Was there too much of me? Was I too cocky? I asked God to please make me only what He wanted me to be, to give me the attitude He wanted me to have the next day.

Yes, when I woke up one eye was swelling. Immediately, I shot a prayer to God: "Thank You, Lord. I needed that. Thank You for *Your* way of answering my prayer." The thanks I felt had not just been a mouthed thanks, but one that welled up from deep within me. Is this what God has been so carefully instructing me to do? Does God know that I am beginning to understand His *gain* when a thank-you automatically wells up within me at the time there is a seeming-*loss*?

Paul's Progression

But Paul's progress was different from mine. Paul's was within the confines of one lesson. He started with one thorn in the flesh. Then when he received a "no" answer, he included more than one physical problem, saying he would glory in his infirmi*ties*—plural (2 Cor. 12:10). Next he came far enough along in the lesson to say he would take pleasure in an expanded list of seeming-losses— reproaches, necessities, persecutions, and distresses. He must have been a better pupil, a more rapid learner than I am. It has taken me years.

In addition to seeing that the Lord would give grace and strength for all his problems and not just his thorn in the flesh, Paul saw two "therefores." They are *because* words.

If Paul's "glorying in his infirmities" stood alone without the "therefore," he would be classed today as a person enjoying his infirmities. *Therefore* points to the reason why Paul said it—because the Lord had answered "No," and had given grace and strength in its place. There is a danger in this kind of glorying, for it tempts people to bring on themselves difficulties in which they can glory. Not Paul. He had prayed repeatedly, expectantly, and fervently for his thorn to be removed *until* his "no" answer, and then he adjusted to it.

"Therefore will I rather glory . . . *[so] that* the power of Christ may rest upon me" (2 Cor. 12:9). What a *gaining*! Paul learned it almost 2,000 years before I learned it, but there it is. One of life's biggest gains for a seeming-loss.

The Lord's "no" answer was actually a great positive which empowered the rest of Paul's ministry. *Gaining through losing*.

The second "therefore" mentioned is in verse 10. "Therefore *I take pleasure* in infirmities, in reproaches, in necessities, in persecutions, in distresses . . ." There is no indication from the scriptural account that Paul *wanted* to lose *so that* he could gain. He not only prayed expectantly, but prayed persistently, repeating three times his prayer that his infirmity would be removed. He didn't invite his losses so that he could receive gains. (However, if we have willfully brought losses upon ourselves, when we ask God to forgive us and let Him take over, He will still bring us gains through them.) But Paul was definitely not getting satisfaction from those difficulties. There is a great gulf between *wanting* losses and *accepting* them, and then receiving the gains which God will give through them.

Paul did not say that he took pleasure in them for themselves, but because he had learned and accepted the *gaining through losing* principle. It was not for his sake. As stated in chapter 1, losing here was also for Christ's sake (v. 10). Taking pleasure—not for his own sake, but for Christ's sake!

California pastor Dr. Tim LaHaye, founder of Family Life Seminars, asked me what the title of my new book was. When I replied, *"Gaining Through Losing,"* a dark scowl crossed his face. Thinking I meant we should *try* to lose so that we can get gains from God, he wisely disagreed with that premise.

"Oh, no, it would be 'sick' to think that way," I agreed. "I do not mean that we deliberately bring losses upon ourselves; but that when they do come—and they come to all of us—then God goes to work in us turning those losses into gains."

Removed Hindrances
I'm fascinated by street sweepers—those massive lumber-

ing machines which loosen and vacuum up debris on the roads. Knowing the magnitude of the task to which the Lord called Paul on the Damascus Road, doesn't it seem logical that He would have sent His supernatural "street cleaner" to dislodge and remove all the hindrances in Paul's pathway? He could have swept the path clean before sending Paul onto it, or at least vacuumed the obstacles *as* they confronted Paul. But the New Testament tells us that God did neither. We see rather that they were left there—deliberately. The whole list which Paul adds to the "infirmities" was left in his path intentionally *so that* he could learn and grow from them. Left *so that* the power would be Christ's omnipotence and not Paul's puny human strength. From man's point of view they were *losses*, but in God's hands they were turned into gigantic *gains*.

I guess the "narrow way" on which Jesus sends me on my journey to heaven hasn't been swept clean either. Even when the source of the annoyance is Satan, as was Job's before the cross and Paul's after the cross, God can and does use that *loss* for *gain* in me too.

Which one of us at some time in life has not wished for, even longed for, a life like Paul's? Full of adventure, fruit, rewards! Changing the world in which he lived! Then influencing people all over Planet Earth! Could the secret be that Paul learned and accepted God's *gaining through losing* principle? God's *so thats*?

What did Paul *lose*? Being delivered from infirmities, reproaches, necessities, persecutions, distresses. What did he *gain*? Christ's grace and power and strength—resting on Him!

Have you discovered God's divine "so that"?

3

What You Can Bear— Your Capacity

In the midst of a deep loss in your life, have you ever cried, "This is more than I can bear"? When a severe financial crisis crashed about you, when shattering news about your health bent you low, or when a calamity in the family sent bitter waves of grief over you, have you felt pressed down till you knew you could not *bear* another minute of it? Years ago I found myself crying out in sorrow after sorrow, "I can't bear it!" Then I decided to find out what the Bible had to say about those crushing times.

As I read the conversation between God and Satan in the Book of Job, it appeared to me that God asked Himself how much Job could *bear*. Then, completely confident of what Job could endure, He gave Satan permission to test him. After Satan left the presence of the Lord the calamities began to fall. Raiding parties and lightning killed or carried off all of Job's animals and his servants, and a desert wind swept down demolishing the house and killing all of his children. Then boils from the soles of his feet to the top of his head left Job mourning in the ashes. The possessions that made Job the greatest man in the East, all of his children, and even his health were *lost*.

As we, like Job, experience testings and trials of varying degrees from time to time, we too feel we cannot bear another minute of the suffering. We ask ourselves what possible *gain* could come out of these horrible *losses*. Seeing the immediate or eventual gain is not only difficult, but often impossible. However, as with Job, there are astounding *gains* for the believer because of his trials and testings.

Job's Capacity

The first comforting *gain* in the midst of Job's difficult losses was his receiving the unconditional confidence of the God of the universe! The Creator knew the stuff of which Job was made. He affirmed Job's *capacity to bear*. God also knew how Job had lived out the qualities in his life thus far, and said to Satan:

Have you considered My servant Job, that there is none like him on the earth, a blameless and upright man, who fears God and turns away from evil? (Job 1:8, RSV)

God also had absolute confidence in Job's future reactions. He trusted Job not only under the ideal conditions of being the greatest man in the East, but also when everything except his life would be taken away from him.

This truth is wonderfully expressed in a New Testament "capacity" promise for those who believe in Christ today when they, as Job, suffer losses in their lives.

God is faithful, who will not suffer *[allow]* you to be tempted *above that you are able;* but will with the temptation also make a way to escape, that you may be able to *bear* it (1 Cor. 10:13).

This is a loving God allowing only what we too can bear—endure.

What a comforting thought for our day that God knows the capacity of the believer, just as He knew Job's! And He will not allow us to be tested above what we can bear. How well He knows the capacity of a Corrie ten Boom and a Joni Eareckson. And He also knows *our* capacity to bear!

What a *privilege* to have God say of us, "There is one of My servants who can stand any testing or trial you can give, Satan!"

Suffering a Compliment?

So we can see that testings and trials are actually a compliment from God. There is not a hint of God questioning Job's ability to withstand and bear. Thus, God could say to Satan, "Everything he has is in your hands, but on the man himself do not lay a finger" (Job 1:12, NIV). God gave Satan permission to do anything except take Job's life. What a confidence in His servant, Job! What a compliment from God!

Last year an extremely fine Christian mother who had just lost her 10-year-old daughter stood weeping in the back hall of a church where I was conducting a seminar. Pressing both my hands in hers, I gently explained that God knew her inmost capacity and what she was strong enough to bear. "So," I told her, "this is actually a compliment from God to you." I watched her expression change—from grief, to surprise, to a hint of a smile. God's compliment, His trust in her began to fill the void of her loss.

One of my greatest joys as a pastor's wife was explaining to those suffering deep trials the surprising fact that God knew their capacity to bear—then watching the healing begin as they accepted His compliment. Gaining through losing!

God Allowing

God seems to use His knowledge of our capacity to bear to regulate His allowing. I like to think of a complete, unbroken circle representing the permissive will of God—what He allows. Then a dot in the center of the circle represents the believer. Nothing can penetrate the circle of God's permissive will unless God allows it.

In Job's case God could have said "No" to Satan, but He did not. Why did God permit Satan to attack Job? Here again is God's *allowing* role. I like to think of how much simpler and nicer life would be without it! God could have avoided all the trouble Satan brings to this earth.

There is still another "allowing" question that has stumped the experts for generations. When my pastor-husband was to begin a Sunday night series of sermons about Job, he challenged the congregation to read the first chapter and then participate in a "stump the pastor" night with our questions. To generate interest he promised a dollar reward to anyone whose question he could not answer.

On Sunday afternoon our seven-year-old Kurt laboriously plodded his way through the first chapter. Then, that night as my husband was confidently fielding all the questions, Kurt raised his hand. The audience smiled as this little one stood and asked, "Dad, since one of the reasons the Father forsook and could not look on His Son, Jesus, while He was bearing our sins on the cross was because the Father could not look on sin—how come God would let Satan into heaven to talk to Him?"

The congregation exploded with laughter as Chris slowly reached into his billfold, took out a dollar bill and handed it to the grinning little boy. Another one of those "allowing" conundrums in the Bible!

Do you too have some questions you want to ask God about His allowing? I keep telling myself that if *I* were God, *I* would not have allowed those things. But that's why I'm not God! When God finally spoke to Job after his friend stopped talking, God asked, "Who is this that darkens counsel by *words without knowledge?*" (Job 38:2) That word *counsel* here means that God had been dealing with Job, not irresponsibly or haphazardly, but according to His consistent, intelligent design. A loving God allowed acccording to His absolute infallibility.

The amazing fact about God's allowing is that Job had

done nothing to deserve the suffering God allowed to come on him. Sometimes we do suffer because we have broken a natural law or God's law. But not so with Job. Job's friends tried to elicit a confession of sin from him, trying to prove that Job's problems were retribution for his sins. But both Job (who could have been wrong) and God (who could not have been wrong) stubbornly clung to Job's innocence.

It was God who brought up the subject to Satan by saying, "Have you considered My servant Job? There is no one on earth like him; *he is blameless and upright,* a man who fears God and shuns evil" (Job 1:8, NIV, italics added). Then, after the first onslaught of disasters, God repeated these words to Satan, adding, "And he still maintains his integrity, though you incited Me against him to ruin him *without any reason.*" Finally, at the very end of the book, God still confirmed Job's innocence (see Job 42:7).

Yes, this is God *allowing* Satan to pierce through the protective circle of His permissive will to get at one of the choice believers of all history! God allowing suffering! What possible *gain* could there be in that?

Why Allow?
So then I must ask *why* God allowed catastrophe, suffering, and loss in Job's Life. (My husband just said, "Honey, you are tackling one of the greatest theological mysteries of the ages.") Perhaps, but this is the question we all are asking, "Why?"

Could it be *so that* He could *set the stage* for a gain? God in His omniscience knew from the beginning the outcome and the gains He would bring through losses. But whether or not Job's gains could *only* have come through these catastrophes, only God knows—the Bible doesn't tell us.

Was God getting Job's attention *so that* He could reveal Himself to him in a new way? Did it take the loss of Job's human and material possessions and the scraping of his overspreading sores with a piece of pottery on an ash heap—all of this to get his attention? Or was it just God using what He had allowed to bring Job face to face with Himself?

There is a New Testament account in which Jesus seemed to be *setting the stage* for a tremendous gain through a loss. After Mary and Martha, the sisters of Lazarus, had sent for Jesus to heal their brother, Jesus strangely enough waited till Lazarus died. (Even the crowd at Lazarus' tomb questioned if Jesus, who had opened the eyes of the blind, could not have kept *this* man from dying.) Because Jesus was about to reveal a profound truth about Himself, did He deliberately *create the climate* for this revelation by tarrying and thus allowing all the suffering and grief of death? Was He allowing the death *so that* it would set the stage for a revolutionary verbal and visual revelation?

Or was it just that, *since* He had tarried, and thus allowed the natural course of events to proceed, Jesus would *take advantage of the situation?* My husband, now employed by Bethel College, says one of the things he misses most about the pastorate is funerals, because the bereaved are often so tender and open, so willing to listen to God speak to them during grief.

Or perhaps Jesus allowed the agony to *get Martha's attention.* Had Jesus longed to reveal great things to her, but because life was going on as usual had she refused to listen? Martha did not automatically choose the "better part." She was a doer, substituting shopping, cooking, and entertaining the Master for the better—being taught by Him. (The Bible doesn't tell us what profound things Jesus taught Martha's sister, Mary, as she sat at His feet completely absorbed in learning from Him. We only know that she, according to Jesus, anointed Him with oil just before His death because she *alone* understood His death.) Did Jesus have to *allow* Martha to go through something that He could have avoided in order to get her attention?

I too have plenty of opportunities to listen to God. Does

God sometimes have to get my attention through hard things in my life also? Am I, like Martha, too encumbered with the tyranny of the urgent to spend time letting God speak to me through His Word and in quiet prayer—until there is a grief that sends me fleeing to Him? Could it be with me too that the greatest revelations come when the sorrow is the deepest?

Sometimes I wonder if God allowed the Watergate scandal in the United States to get our attention—even after millions of Christians had just fasted and prayed all day that April 30 in 1974. We suddenly became the Ugly Americans overseas, lost our national self-respect, and saw ourselves as we really were. But God had our attention! It was for many the beginning of the turning to Him for direction and the coming out into the open on the part of millions of silent Christians. God *allowing* to get our attention?

Whatever the reason for the allowing in the death of Lazarus, the fact remains that Jesus deliberately allowed death and grief which He could have averted. Although we may not understand, Jesus knew His "why"—the gains He would bring through the loss.

During her loss, Jesus gave Martha—a common, ordinary, domestically inclined woman friend—one of the greatest announcements that Planet Earth has ever received:

"I AM THE RESURRECTION AND THE LIFE!"

That proclamation from Jesus must have sent her grieving heart reeling and her throbbing head spinning. Then He proved the credibility of this startling message by calling forth the deceased one before the eyes of the stunned crowd. I remember standing in awe at the small ground-level opening to Lazarus' tomb just outside Jerusalem, wondering what kind of power had propelled that body, bound from head to foot, out of that cramped cavity in that hillside.

But the world-changing impact was not made by Jesus'

tremendous display of power in raising Lazarus from the dead. Although he was resuscitated, Lazarus would eventually die again. Also, Jesus had already raised another without this kind of impact. But the power of that moment was that Jesus was declaring and proving that He Himself really *is* the Resurrection and the Life. No other religion on earth offers this! And, in living and walking on earth among them after He also had died, Jesus proved that I too shall live again (see 1 Cor. 15).

He hadn't tarried too long! Jesus knew His "why" for allowing Martha's sorrow all along! What a fantastic *gain* for Martha. What a privilege—in her *loss*—to be the one used by the Master to reveal the greatest news ever to reach Planet Earth!

Job's Gains from His Losses
So now we turn again to Job's gains through his losses. In addition to God's confidence in what he could bear, Job's gains were many.

The most obvious gain was in *what God restored* to Job. Twice as much as he had before! Fourteen thousand in place of seven thousand sheep and goats; six thousand camels replacing three thousand lost ones; one thousand yoke of oxen in the place of five hundred; a thousand female donkeys to replace five hundred. His lost children were replaced with seven more sons and three more daughters—these fairer than all the women in the whole land. Then Job was given another 140 years to live and see his children's children to the fourth generation. *Gaining through losing.*

But in our concentrating on what God restored to Job, we fail to see all the *gains* throughout the suffering of the *losses*. Did God allow Job's suffering simply to show him that He could restore twofold? I think not.

The key to the Book of Job is seen by many to be Job's statement in chapter 23, verse 10: "When He has tried me, I shall come forth as gold." There are several possible gains which could be inferred in this declaration by Job. The first is the *purifying power of affliction*—God allowing suffering to strengthen Job and purify him as precious refined gold. God producing the patience through trials for which Job is so well known (James 5:11). Suffering producing purer gold! How I have clung to this outcome of God's dealings in my own life since my early 20s. How I have seen myself, and then my husband and my children, grow and stretch during times of affliction.

But there is another possible meaning in this great verse. Another gain—*the vindicating power of affliction*. Was Job vindicating his innocence, clearing his name? Was he saying to his accusing friends, "You'll see. When God is done trying me, you will know that I really hadn't been sinning against Him. It will be proved that I have been good all along."

Then the gain spoken of in Job 23:10 might also be the *proving of his faith through suffering*. Though Job's complaint came through in his speeches during his suffering, he never lost his unequivocal and unshakable faith in God. In reply to his friends' accusations, he stubbornly defended his relationship with and faith in the God who was allowing all his suffering. In the midst of their accusations Job cried out, *"Though He slay me, yet will I hope in Him"* (Job 13:15, NIV). "The God who is allowing all this testing is still my God!"

What a lesson has come to us down through the ages. Job declared to himself, his friends, and to all future generations that no matter what happened, his faith in his God was unshakable!

As I have been reading the Book of Job while at work on this manuscript, God keeps bringing to my mind a gain tucked down in the last chapter—the *when of restoration*. It was *after* Job prayed for the friends who had given him wrong advice and accused him in his sorrow that God restored Job's possessions. God finally told Job's friends that He was angry with them for not telling the truth about Him; and that, after their burnt offering was made, "My servant Job will pray for you, and I will accept his prayer and not deal with you according to your folly" (Job 42:8, NIV).

God, the great Psychiatrist! How much change of attitude it must have taken Job to be willing to pray *for* his friends. Did God give a *principle* here that we are just now discovering in modern psychiatry and Christianity? I have seen it happen so many times in my own life that when I get my mind off *my* troubles and concentrate on *praying for others*—that much is restored to me—emotionally, physically, and spiritually. Gaining through losing!

Another tremendous gain for Job came in his learning to *discern the voices*. First he learned not to accept all the advice of his well-meaning friends. Job firmly resisted their assumed omniscience. Perhaps the kindest thing Job's friend did for him during his sorrow was just to sit with him for seven days—in silence. For when they did speak, God summed up their long speeches with, "You have not spoken of Me what is right" (Job 42:7, NIV).

Often I find myself desperately grasping at advice from others when I am deeply hurting. How easy it is for me to listen to their "reasoning." But how important for me too to sort out the truth from their sometimes misguided help.

Then at times the voice I hear in my sorrow is not that of another, but, like Job, it is my own. My voice of self-pity. Or self-justification—when I am trying to convince *myself* of my innocence. Or sometimes it is my own voice of self-defensiveness against what others are saying. But I cannot see myself clearly while in the depth of my sorrows, for my tear-filled vision distorts my perspective and thus the advice I give myself. My interpretation of the Bible becomes distorted. I find a focus that soothes and smoothes me—but fails to help me see clearly the truth about myself.

However, the greatest *gain* of all came when Job stopped listening to his own voice and *put his hand over his mouth.* When God finally answered, Job cried, "Behold, I am insignificant; what can I reply to Thee? I *lay my hand on my mouth*" (Job 40:4, NASB). It was when Job finally learned to keep still that his greatest gain came—he heard God!

Yes, Job heard the God of the universe in a fresh and new revelation of His grandeur and power never before heard on Planet Earth! There were no books or other resources to enlighten Job at that early date in history. But God showed Job the animate and inanimate wonders of the universe. Then when Job finally heard the True One speaking, he saw himself from an accurate perspective for the first time. God gently yet firmly chided him as a parent questioning his offspring, "Where were you when I laid the foundation of the earth?" (38:4, NASB) The defensive, argumentative Job had no answer. Having seen himself in contrast to God, he lowered his accusing voice to whisper, "I am of no account."

Yes, it was when the human strife of words was over that Job's greatest gain came—He had heard God! And Job put his hand over his mouth.

Surprisingly, after all of Job's trials, when God did speak, He spoke out of a whirlwind and out of a storm. Hadn't Job had enough problems without God speaking out of a storm? But somehow I too find that God doesn't usually speak out of the soft, gentle breezes to me. It is in the storms that He speaks in very special ways to me as He did to Job in his distress and to Martha in her severe storm.

This does not mean that God never speaks in the calm. As a young woman and I sat in my mother's porch swing this past summer, she asked, "Is there something wrong with me that I'm not suffering? I've never really suffered." (Yet some people might say she was, for she had been serving Christ in evangelism for two years without pay!)

I assured her, "No, you are in the circumstances God wants you in now. Suffering may come. Just prepare yourself in your relationship with Him in prayer and Bible study so that if the suffering does come you will be ready. Job knew God to the best of his ability *before* his suffering. Just be sure you know God well enough to *hear* and *recognize* His voice if and when the storm comes."

But I believe one of the most beautiful gains for Job came in the *fulfilling of a wish*—wishing that his words would be preserved for posterity, not on parchment which would decay, but on stone with iron—forever. At the low point in his life, when things looked the blackest, Job cried: "Oh, that my words were recorded, that they were written on a scroll, that they were inscribed with an iron tool on lead, or engraved in rock forever" (19:23-24, NIV).

Then came his spontaneous burst of unshakable faith:

I know that my Redeemer lives, and that in the end He will stand upon the earth. And after my skin has been destroyed, yet in my flesh I will see God" (vv. 25-26, NIV).

Centuries before Jesus revealed to Martha the secrets of resurrection, which we read in the Bible today, Job tenaciously and unwaveringly clung to the certainty of living after death. Preserved through all the ages, for all generations of suffering saints—in the world's all-time number one best-seller—the Bible. Job's wish was granted!

We have an unannounced contest in our family—who gets Christmas going earliest—the first gift purchased—the first decoration displayed. At our recent October family birthday dinner, Skip, one my sons-in-law, announced, "Ev won. She has already listened to *The Messiah!*"

But I don't just *listen* to Handel's *Messiah*. I *feel* it! That day I had turned the volume up so that the whole house reverberated with, "I *know* that my Redeemer liveth!" Thousands of years after Job! Then the exploding crescendos that have brought concert goers to their feet since the 19th century: "Hallelujah, Hallelujah . . . and He shall reign for ever and ever!"

What would Christmas be without Handel's *Messiah*?

But what would his *Messiah* be without Job? And what would Job be without suffering?

Although Job didn't know I would even be born, his words have been preserved just for me. A decade ago a deep tragedy happened to one of our children which I still cannot share. That crushing event which came into my life as a parent should have left me bleeding and broken. But just today as I was leafing through the Bible I had used during that calamity, I discovered I had written the name of the child to whom it happened in the margin of that Bible by Job 19:25, not with Job's questioning, or with his complaining—but with his outburst of undefeatable faith. "I *know* that my Redeemer liveth!" In *my* storm I had echoed Job's unshakable faith!

But Job's experience was not recorded just for my big, earth-shattering disasters. Last night I came to the end of a particularly frustrating day. Each succeeding phone call ended with a "wait until something else gets straightened out." As the evening bore down on me with frustration, tenseness, and inner sputtering, I absentmindedly flicked on the record player as I walked by. Suddenly the whole house was alive again with "I *know* that my Redeemer liveth!"

The transformation was instantaneous. My negative attitudes melted. My whole being was soaring, praising, and worshiping—God! Job's wish was fulfilled again.

What fantastic *gains because of* Job's horrible *losses*. Gains Job could not have even dreamed possible. Were Job's *gains* worth his *losses*? Who would even dare ask God that question?

"Who" Not "Why"

Have you ever asked "Why" during your trials? Neither Martha's nor Job's "why" questions were ever completely answered, and the mystery of the drama of heaven between God and Satan was never revealed to Job.

But whatever the reason for God's allowing of the grief

really doesn't matter—for it was in their sorrows that God chose to reveal Himself in new and magnanimous ways. As I settled down to once again read of the way God revealed Himself to Job in the 38th and 39th chapters, God kept getting bigger and bigger and bigger. How Job must have felt himself shrinking and shrinking as his knowledge of God kept expanding and expanding—*who He is*.

It was when God finished giving Job the new revelation of who He really was that Job could cry, "My ears had heard *of* You, but now my eyes have seen You" (Job 42:5, NIV). Then Job suddenly knew all was well with him and with the whole universe! God was, and always has been, in control. The combatant turned into the worshiper. And all of Job's "whys" turned to "Who."

I had lunch recently with Arvella Schuller, wife of Dr. Robert Schuller of the "Hour of Power" telecast from Garden Grove, Calif. I was amazed and thrilled as she radiantly smiled and kept reaffirming the gains that had come through her recent losses—the motorcycle accident in which her beautiful, vivacious daughter Carol's life was hanging by a thread before the leg amputation; endless, exhausting daily therapy; and in the midst of it all, the verdict of her own cancer, and the surgery which followed. She summed it all up by saying that when people say that it certainly must have been a rough year, she replies, "Oh no. It has been a blessed year filled with the presence of God and surrounded by the loving arms of many people." Then she added, "Evelyn, I saw a different side of God's face, and it was tremendous!"

During the first years of my marriage, I found myself almost drowning in a sea of "why" questions as trials flooded over me —and I just knew I could not bear them. But gradually I detected an emerging pattern. It was in those times of engulfment in a sea of sorrows that God would speak to me in a new way. Little by little I saw it. God was choosing to reveal Himself to me at those times, in each instance showing me a deeper, more profound side of Himself—one I'd never seen before.

One of my author-friends who is in my personal prayer group, after I had asked for prayer for God's will in overseas ministries invitations, commented, "You really do live a 'Cinderella' existence, don't you?"

Taken aback, I replied, "If I do live a life like 'Cinder Ella,' now, it's because I've spent so many years on the *ash* heap with Job!"

It has been many, many years since I have asked God "why" in my trials. With a shocking report from a doctor, a calamity in a child's life, or some shattering news in the family, I find myself searching for that "more of my God—my Who. I, with Job, have heard much *of* God, but it has always been in those difficult times of my life that I have seen Him—ready and eager to reveal more of Himself to me. What a fabulous *gain* through my *losses!*

Have your "whys" turned to "Who"?

4

What You Can Bear— Your Potential

There is another meaning of the word *bear* in the Bible. This time not only what we are *able* to bear—our CAPACITY, but how much we *can* bear—our POTENTIAL. God knew how much Job could stand, but Jesus explained another use of this word—how much we can produce.

As we rode to a seminar in California last winter, my hostess and I passed field after field of ugly, bleeding stumps with wires strung above them. Finally I asked her, "What on earth are those?"

"Oh," she said with obvious pride, "they're our grapevines!"

As I gazed on them in silence, my heart cried out to God, "Father, am I that ugly when You are pruning me?"

God of the Grapes
Jesus' words from John 15 kept whirling around in my mind. "I am the true Vine, and My Father is the Vinedresser. . . . Every branch that beareth fruit, He purgeth it . . . (John 15:1-2, sco). It is the Father, said Jesus, who holds the pruning knife in His hand and prunes those who are His own. How I cringed at this vivid example in those vineyards of that seldom-mentioned concept of

God—bending over us, cutting away—The Vinedresser.

I found a little consolation in Jesus' assuring words that it is only the branches who are vitally, organically connected to Him (not just those who go to church or follow His ethics and teachings) whom the Father prunes.

But as Jesus' words kept marching through my mind like the rows of vines flashing past our car, a surprising thought emerged: it is those of us who are already bearing fruit whom God prunes! So why the pruning process? *So that* we can bear—not just *some* fruit—but *more* fruit!

It was winter in California when I was glimpsing those ugly stumps from the car window. Suddenly God showed me there are winters in my life too. In fact, He said, as with grapes, all the seasons are represented in our lives also. But not necessarily one following the other in predictable solar-induced regularity. Usually they tumble unscheduled according to the needs we have as human branches.

But I don't like some seasons. I hate dormant periods when the "sap" has retreated, and sadly there doesn't seem to be much happening through me. Then there is the growing season, that time when I'm being fed and nourished by the Vine when the fruit is ripening and I spoil it by impatiently straining to pluck it. I certainly don't care for the pruning season when the wielding of that sharp knife mercilessly prunes away the abundant leaves and long stems of my just-past time of productivity. No, I definitely prefer the glorious, rewarding fruit-bearing season.

Then I wondered about God. Does His heart bleed with the branch when He knows the only way to produce more fruit is to get out His pruning knife? Does it hurt Him more than it hurts me? Does He like the fruit-bearing season best too?

Mentally I dug into my past losses—sorrow, suffering, lost babies, surgery, family difficulties—and wondered if some, or many of them, had occurred because God had put his pruning tools to work. I had definitely been left feeling like a bare, bleeding stump after those experiences. Yes, I had been pruned by the hand of the divine Vine-dresser!

Touched by God

I have been touched by the hand of God in so many different ways. I've felt His strong supporting hand beneath me when I've crumpled in grief. Have been securely held in the hollow of His hand when life engulfed me. When there was no power of my own, I've felt the omnipotence of His hand. I've known His firm hand steering the course of my life. Experienced the restraining of His hand when I would run ahead. Felt the tenderness of the divine Gardener's hand pressing mine. I've been made well by the touch of the hand of the Great Physician. And I've felt His cooling hand on my hot feverish brow. But I have also felt the sting of the pruning knife in the omniscient Vine-dresser's hand.

Somehow in our imaginations we have invented a God whose hand gives only love pats. But this is not what the Bible tells us. Job, at the low ebb in his suffering, cried, "The hand of God hath touched me" (Job 19:21). Paul, after being touched by God on the Damascus Road, was blinded for a season. Jacob, before he crossed the Jabbok River to be reunited with his estranged brother, Esau, wrestled and felt the touch of God on his thigh, and he was permanently crippled—by God. As the sinew shrank, Jacob said, "I have seen *God* face to face" (Gen. 32:30).

The place where I felt God's presence the most while touring the Holy Land was at the Jabbok River where Jacob had wrestled all night. I slipped away down the bank and sat alone, motionless, absorbing every bit of that Presence. The surrounding hills formed a natural amphitheater; and reverberating, echoing across the valley from hill to hill—God!

I pondered in that place: *Was losing the full use of a part of his physical body and limping for the rest of his life worth what*

Jacob gained? The answer was overwhelmingly "Yes." Personally blessed by God! Blessed beyond his fondest dreams. Then given a new name. Not Supplanter now, but Israel. "A nation and a company of nations shall be of thee, and kings shall come out of thy loins" (35:11). And he was given power with God—and power with men.

Wrestling

I too have wrestled spiritually with the Lord and felt the surprising result of having a leg touched by God. Because of frequent questions by Christians who had sometimes seen God heal physically and sometimes not, I fervently and persistently prayed during the summer of 1977 that God would give me His answers. Then in September I prayed, "God, teach me everything about healing that I need to know." Once again He used my own body to teach me what I had prayed for. In October the process started.

I had come home from a speaking engagement in the Bahamas with a severe virus which had attacked the nerve roots of my spine. Ten days later, as I left for the East Coast for three upcoming seminars, I wondered if I could handle the pain. One morning after struggling with the almost unbearable task of getting my nylons over my toes, I stood up, stopped attempting to get ready for the seminar—and wrestled with God. "Lord," I prayed, "either take this pain away—or give me the grace to stand it."

To my astonishment, the excruciating pain began to lessen, and in a few minutes had all but vanished. But, even more surprising, my left leg went limp. I dragged myself up the stairs to breakfast and stood on my "good" leg for the five hours of speaking on that day, and for many seminars after that one. Touched by God!

Much of our wrestling is *against* God. There is a difference when we wrestle *with* Him. Jacob wrestled *with* God until He blessed him. Davy, in *A Severe Mercy*, wrestled all night with God, giving Him herself for His will in her life (Sheldon Vanauken, Harper and Row, p. 146). So I too was wrestling *with* God until He had His will in me.

As I look back at two years of wrestling with this leg problem, I realize that not once did I wrestle *against* God. The whole experience has been without rebellion of any kind. I couldn't always say that about previous physical problems. I was in complete rebellion against being on the shelf during that hospitalization for gallbladder surgery —until the sweet joy of surrender to His will came after hearing the poem "Gaining Through Losing" over the air.

Contending with the swollen eyes has been a series of gradual learning of God's *so thats*. But not with this leg. These months have been so different—not always understanding why, but always knowing God knew why and what He was doing. So the wrestling has been with Him—to gain all He has for me. Wrestling as Jacob wrestled, over and over again *until He blesses me*—and gives me what He wanted to give me all along.

How did wrestling and being touched by the divine Vinedresser produce blessings in me? The only time I shed tears while still in the hospital was when I had to face the cancellation of a large seminar in another state. But God had more fruit in mind all along. I had no choice but to send another person in my place—Loree, a close prayer associate whom God had been marvelously preparing for years for that very task. And the great results of her seminar proved that God was doubling my prayer ministry here in the United States.

Then I saw another "why." With Loree's teaching, God released me from the total ministry here to permit me to begin an overseas ministry to which He had called me for two years. More fruit—when pruned!

The Expert Pruner
Recently my friend Jane brought me a small purple passion plant which she had started from her own. While I was anxiously waiting for it to grow in its new environ-

ment, it suddenly shot straight up, resembling a purple and green bean pole. Common sense told me to pinch off the top, but I could not muster the courage. For several weeks I approached it, fingers poised, only to lose my nerve and retreat. I could not bear to hurt my little plant. Finally I steeled myself, gritted my teeth, and pinched. To my surprise, in just one week many new shoots appeared on the stalk, filling out the ugly leafless spots. But later when I returned from a speaking tour, to my horror, a long sprout had shot out from the top at a very awkward angle, and the main stem had compensated by bending in the opposite direction to keep from falling over. Again I resolutely gathered all my courage—and pinched. Then I came to one conclusion—I am not an expert pruner. I just don't know how to do it.

I learned at my last California seminar that it takes an expert to prune effectively. The wife of a grape grower said to me, "Do you want to know something about pruning? Very few people can prune. We go to great trouble to hire the very best expert available."

God is the Expert Pruner. The supernatural divine Professional. He never pinches or cuts too soon lest He damage my tender branch. He never lets me get too far out of control before he draws His knife. He knows just how far to let me sprawl. He understands which part of me and just exactly how much of that part He must prune. How precious to know that the care of me as Jesus' branch will never have to be entrusted to a human vinedresser. My Vinedresser is an Expert. He is God.

He's Sovereign

Since *pruning* means "purging by removal," "cleansing by separation from," and "cutting away living parts," we must ask, does God just *allow* or does He actually *do something* that hurts His own? Here we have one of the theological battles of the ages.

During my son Kurt's first summer, before he learned to

walk, I would put him out in our sunny backyard to play. The first thing we had done after moving into our parsonage on a main street was to fence in the backyard and secure the gates with locks to protect our children from that busy traffic. One day I answered a ring at the front door and a stranger stood holding our Kurt in her arms. "Is this your baby? I found him crawling into State Street." I numbly reached out and took him from her arms, too shocked to do more than mumble a weak "thank-you" as she turned and disappeared.

I've thought of that stranger often. What if she *hadn't* rescued that little one from the relentless stream of traffic? Would she have *caused* his death? Who would have been responsible for it? An older neighbor-child who had unlocked the gate? The mother for trusting the fence and locks? Or the woman who could have snatched him from the wheels of the cars? We would say—the one who deliberately allowed the child to be hit. The one who was fully aware of the danger and had the power to avert the tragedy.

Is it so with God? Since He has the power and ability to stop any difficulty in our lives, what is His part? Most people can agree that God allows suffering but feel that His sending unpleasant or difficult things into our lives is inconsistent with His being a God of love.

The writer of the Book of Hebrews states that God *was able* to save His Son, Jesus, from the death of the cross (Heb. 5:7). Jesus even cried with strong tears to His Father who *was able to save Him*. But God did not. It was God the Father's will that His Son should suffer and die. (We know that technically Satan caused Christ's death when he brought sin into the world and made the redemption on the cross necessary.) But God could have chosen a less severe method of redemption. God could also have prevented Job's suffering by saying "No" to Satan and not allowing the suffering, but He did not. Jesus could have prevented Lazarus' death and thus avoided Martha's suffering. But He did not. So did He cause Job's and Martha's grief?

To be sure, I sometimes bring suffering upon myself. When I break God's moral or physical laws carelessly or deliberately, I must reap the consequences. Sometimes sorrow is the result of a natural course of events here on this fallen planet. But sometimes it is of God. God defended Job when his friends declared that Job's suffering was the consequence of sin. The Old Testament abounds with instances of God sending affliction (see Num. 14:28, 33; Pss. 66:10-11; 119:71, 75: Isa. 9:1). Our preconceived ideas about God may not be consistent with what His Word says about Him.

At Bethel College's 1980 Founder's Week, I witnessed two vivid examples of God choosing not to prevent suffering. One of our speakers, Cliff Barrows, pulled an object from his pocket and showed us one of his most precious possessions—a glass eye. It was given to him by his close friend and associate, blind singer Kim Wickes, who had gotten a new one.

Then I watched the U.S. Army chief of chaplains place the Order of Aaron and Hur medallion (the highest honor bestowed by the chaplain's corps) around the neck of one of my husband's dearest friends, retired commandant of the U.S. Army chaplain school, Chester Lindsey. This great Christian was in the final stage of cancer. And my heart cried out to God, "You can—why don't You—give Kim *real* eyes and Chet that healthy, vibrant body we used to know?"

But such questions aren't for Christians to ask. We must not only look past the losses to the gains, but we *must see the real God at work.*

At a convention this past summer, I asked Joni Eareckson if she would give me a quote for this book. She cheerily responded, "Sure. Come to my room when I'm through speaking tonight." Still in braces from her shoulders to her hands and feet, she lay on her bed talking to me about questioning God and praying to be healed from the paralysis which resulted from her diving accident. Then she wistfully recounted her gradual climb up through those reactions to her present beautiful relationship with God. As we discussed whether God just allowed these things or actually had a part in sending them, she suddenly broke forth in a beaming smile and exclaimed, "Oh, that isn't even a good question, is it? *He's sovereign!* He's in control of everything!"

Joni—the one I had seen the year before receiving an award at the national Christian Bookseller's Convention for being the Number One author reaching today's Christian teenagers. Why? *Because* of her tragic accident!

Sovereign! The expert, supernatural Vinedresser who gives the perfect season, the perfect nourishment, the perfect protection, and the perfect pruning—to His precious branches.

Fruit

By now are you saying you don't want any part of a God like that? Are you thinking, *With a friend like that, who needs enemies?* James explained in his epistle that when we can look back and see what the Lord has brought about through suffering, we will realize that He really was good all along.

> Brothers, as an example of patience in the face of suffering, take the prophets who spoke in the name of the Lord. As you know, we consider blessed those who have persevered. You have heard of Job's perseverance and have seen what the Lord finally brought about. The Lord is full of compassion and mercy (James 5:10-11, NIV).

Jesus explained that God's reason for pruning is never to hurt us but to produce more fruit. That glorious season we love so much. *Fruit-bearing!* Accomplished by God's all-loving, all-wise process!

Fruit? What is fruit in our lives? In the New Testament, fruit occasionally means the winning of souls. But usually it means what is produced in our personality—*our potential.* Those visible expressed character traits which the Holy Spirit produces in us—"love, joy, peace, long-suffering, gentleness, goodness, faith, meekness, self control" (Gal. 5:22-23).

I recall how I busily jotted notes at Urbana '70 as Dr. John Stott explained that *fruitfulness* almost always means "Christlikeness." I wrote this quotation from him: "Pruning—pain, sorrow, suffering, frustrated ambition, grief. Much of our suffering is the chastening of Hebrews 12:10, *'That we may share in His holiness'"* (NIV).

It is amazing to study Scripture and see *how* these personality gains are produced. James wrote, "My brethren, count it all joy when you fall into various trials, knowing this, that the testing of your faith worketh patience. But let patience have her perfect work that you may be perfect and entire, lacking nothing" (James 1:2-4, SCO). Our potential is fulfilled through trials. Paul wrote, "But we glory in tribulations also; knowing that tribulation worketh patience; and patience, experience; and experience, hope" (Rom. 5:3-4). Penned beside Romans 8:28 ("All things work together for good. . . .") in my old Bible is the simple, now fading word, "Judy," the child we lost in infancy, with an arrow pointing to the pruning verse John 15:2. Pruned! For my good. To produce fruit—more Christlikeness—in me.

In California I was told that if grapes are not pruned, a fuzzy, ugly, hairlike growth appears on the branches of the vine. I may think everything being produced in my life is the luscious fruit of the Spirit. But God, seeing the real me, gets out His pruning knife and cuts away at the branches.

There are many extensive and expensive courses being taught these days to help people discover their full potential. But God's 2,000-year-old formula has been available to us all along. And through it—*gained—the rare privilege of actually realizing our full potential!*

Spiritual Fruit of the Womb

But as mentioned previously, there are some examples in the Bible of the other kind of fruit being produced in our lives. There is the fruit of the womb—spiritual offspring. This comes as a result of "bearing" a witness (see John 15:27). Jesus told His disciples, "Lift up your eyes, and look on the fields; for they are white already to harvest, and he that reapeth . . . gathereth *fruit* unto life eternal" (John 4:35-36). With this same idea, Paul expressed his desire to visit the Romans that he might have some *fruit* among them (see Rom. 1:13).

It was because of Mary and Martha's grief that Jesus had the opportunity to demonstrate His power at the grave of Lazarus which produced the fruit of souls. "Many of the Jews who came to Mary [and Martha], and had seen the things which Jesus did, believed on Him" (John 11:45; see also 12:11).

Recently a woman wrote, "Dear Evelyn, I am really going to watch for your next book, *Gaining Through Losing.* I gained through losing my husband. . . . He was fatally injured by his chain saw. . . . My five children ranged in age from 21 months to 15 years. . . . It's a long story how the Lord used Ron's death to bring us all back to California, and how, *one by one, each of us came to Him.*" Eternal fruit!

At an annual convention of the auxiliary of the Home World Bible League in one of Chicago's large motels, the previous manager had overbooked. As a result 2,000 women waited for hours in tedious lines for rooms, some being shuttled to less desirable hotels and arriving back late for meetings. Torrential rain had flooded the below-ground-level convention room. Just two hours before the first session began, maintenance people had siphoned two inches of water from the floor. The 94-degree temperature and an inadequate air-conditioning system for a crowd that size had turned the room into a literal steam bath. Disaster reigned.

Just before I closed the last session, the new manager asked for time on our program. After explaining that his predecessor had lost his job because of the frightful over-booking, he thanked those ladies profusely for their beautiful spirit all that weekend. "If I had had this many traveling salesmen, they would have been fistfighting in the halls over the rooms. But not one of you complained once." Then—to thunderous applause—he said, "In fact, ladies, you have made a believer out of me!"

Gained—the privilege of being one of the branches God chooses to prune—*so that* I can realize my full potential of what I can be—*so that* I can bear eternal fruit!

God is Good?
Back in 1943 my mother-in-law, 42 years old with two young children and a grown son away at war, answered the phone early one morning. It was the family doctor bearing the message that her husband, recovering from minor surgery, had just been found dead in his hospital bed. Being in the room with her, I listened in awe to her spontaneous response to that shocked doctor: "I still say God is good."

Yes, God *is* good. "But though He causes grief; yet will He have compassion according to the multitude of His mercies. For He doth not afflict willingly" (Lam. 3:32-33). But *His pruning is always to develop our full potential!*

Looking back at God's dual role of allowing and causing in my life, can I still say I love him? Yes, with Job I can truthfully say, "Though He slay me, yet will I trust in Him" (Job 13:15). But at 4 o'clock the other morning, a thought occurred to me. *After all the pruning seasons in my life where God seemingly left me a bleeding, ugly stump, do I still* like *Him?*

There is quite a difference between my loving God and

liking what He does. But even after all these years that God has allowed testing and has actually pruned me (admittedly to bear fruit), do I still *like* Him?

I wiggled down under the blankets, a smile crept over my face, and I exclaimed, "Hey, God I really *do* like You!"

In the light of your understanding God's roles of both allowing and doing the testing in your life, do *you* still like Him?

Do you like God— or just love Him?

5

Aloneness

Aloneness—the result of one of the greatest losses we can experience—that sometimes sudden and ever-deepening realization that we have been deprived of human companionship. The loss may come through death, separation, divorce, rebellion, or distance.

Aloneness is serious, frequently producing mild to severe physical, emotional, or mental stress. Numerous studies cite a definite correlation between loneliness and frequency of illness, length of hospitalization, admission to mental institutions, and a higher death rate. Writing on this subject, Dr. James J. Lynch, psychologist at the University of Maryland School of Medicine in Baltimore, states:

> Individuals who live alone—widows and widowers, divorced and single people—may be particularly vulnerable to stress and anxiety because they continuously lack the tranquilizing effect of human companionship (*The Broken Heart: The Medical Consequences of Loneliness*, Basic Books).

Since the loss of human companionship at sometime in life is inescapable, must the inevitable result always be complete loss for us? Must we endure these shattering losses alone? Is there no one to take up the role of companionship, to produce a tranquility in us?

Yes, there is. Jesus. He is the One who promised those who love Him, "Lo, I am with you alway, even unto the end of the world" (Matt. 28:20). Always and forever! Companionship with Him is always available to us. He will never forsake His own, never rupture the relationship, never sever the bonds of love.

But there is still another dimension in aloneness for the Christian. There is the hope of actually *gaining* through the *losing* of human companionship.

God Comes in Proportion to Our Needs

Theologians tell us that God is omnipresent, that is, He has the ability to be everywhere at once. But does this mean He is in all places at all times in the same proportion? It does not appear so.

An amazing characteristic of God's nature that I have observed is: *He always comes in proportion to our needs.* The deeper the sorrow, the more comfort He gives; the larger the void, the more God fills it; the greater the need, the more we have of Him. "The Lord is *nigh* unto them that are of a broken heart"(Ps. 34:18).

I have found in my own life that God always comes in proportion to my need. It is more than just, "Lo, I am with you alway." That is God's "when"—always! But there are differences in my "whens." Difficult circumstances require an added measure of this strength and grace. At those times I can be sure He will be with me in that same proportion.

There is a quality and a seeming quantity of His presence that changes with life's needs. It is like the "as" of Moses' beautiful promise to Asher during his final benediction to the 12 tribes which has been a comfort to every succeeding generation of believers: "As thy days, so shall thy strength be" (Deut. 33:25). More strength is given when more strength is needed!

Sharing some ideas for this book with Joni Eareckson last summer, I told her about God always coming in proportion to our needs. Lying on a bed in her braces, she became quiet, pondered my statement, and then said, "Oh, that really ministers to me, Evelyn."

A woman in her 30s came to me in a large Midwestern church with a horrifying story: "My husband seemingly went out of his mind temporarily and beat me with a hammer, trying to kill me. The excruciating pain was almost more than I could bear. Nobody was around to help me in that awful moment. But in that terrifying aloneness, something astounding happened. I saw Jesus standing right by me. I was not alone!"

As I listened, there welled up within me a sudden longing to actually see Jesus like that. I had never seen Him in that way. But then I realized—I've never needed Him to that extent either. However, the premise still is true. He has always come to the degree that I have needed Him—in proportion to my need!

This knowledge has given me a wonderful assurance for the future, since through all these years He has never failed to come in the exact proportion to my need. I can face whatever life may bring, little problems or huge tragedies, and know absolutely that Jesus will be there in the exact ratio to my need.

When we *lose* the security and help of human companionship, the *gain* we experience is that fantastic proportion in which God gives of Himself to us. It was in a hospital that I first learned this concept. Hospitalization produces a particular kind of aloneness—the loss of the security of all familiar human companionship. Absent too are all the familiar sounds, smells, and sights of our usual surroundings.

The night before surgery brings a very special kind of aloneness. I was just 34 when I entered a hospital for my first surgery. A lump in each breast foreshadowed an al-

most certain verdict of cancer. I had an overwhelming
need—and God knew it.

After my husband and all the hospital personnel had
left me, an amazing thing happened. It was not just that I
was opening myself up to Him more, but I could suddenly
sense God actually filling that stark, white room with
Himself. As I lay on that bed, I was acutely aware of His
presence permeating the room right up to the corners of
the ceiling. He was there—all that I needed of Him. More
of Him than I could ever remember experiencing before.
*God understood the magnitude of my need, and came accord-
ingly.*

When the chaplain came for his usual cheer-up-tomor-
row's surgery-rites, I didn't need him. Perhaps he didn't
appreciate God usurping his rights, but God had already
come!

What a *gain* in that *losing* situation! *Gained*—that unique
privilege of having my room filled with the overwhelming
presence of the God of the universe! The God even the
heaven of the heavens cannot contain! And *gained*—the
lifelong realization that no matter how great my need,
God will infuse it to the extent that it needs filling. God
coming in proportion to my need! Although the next day's
surgery proved the tumors to be benign, I had learned one
of life's most important lessons.

Through my years as a pastor's wife I have assured apprehensive, frightened, hospitalized friends that it was a
privilege—yes, a privilege—for them to be in that hospital
with a very deep need—because they too could experience His coming in proportion to that need. What do we
gain when we *lose* all familiar human support? More of
God!

But my third surgery—gallbladder—produced a surprise for me. At 4 A.M., just 12 hours before check-in time
at the hospital, I was facing a frustrating schedule of last-
minute loads of washing, the final mopping of the kitchen
floor, the preparation of food to be stored in the refriger-

ator—wondering how I could ever get it all done before 4
P.M. As I lay beside my husband in the silence of the pre-
dawn darkness, I cried out to God in my special need:
"God, I'm leaving my little ones, my home . . . so much
undone . . . surgery!" Then I felt God coming in a powerful, but different way than He had come before the previous surgery. He was so real that I almost felt myself lifted
and mingled with Him. I spent a long time just lingering
in this precious presence—finding strength, comfort,
encouragement. All the things I needed so badly for that
day.

Then I shook Chris and woke him exclaiming, "Oh,
Honey, God came early this time!"

Chris smiled and held me close. "He must have known
you needed Him early this time." Of course, He did. He
had come in proportion to my need—again!

So once again I learned the lesson. Now as I reflect on
the gentle progression of God teaching me through hospital experiences, I realize that this principle had been in
operation without my recognizing it all of my Christian
life—God coming in proportion to my need.

Death: When God Severs a Human Relationship

The greatest aloneness we ever experience is in the violent
rending of loved ones by death. The loss is gargantuan.
Almost unimaginable. *Can God, does* He come in *that* great
a proportion?

My first years of marriage seemed to be full of losses.
Death was everywhere. Losing at three months the un-
planned baby conceived on our honeymoon produced a
psychological and, surprisingly, physical void entailing an
adjustment that for me was deeper than any postpartum
blues I later experienced—a body shocked at premature
loss. Aloneness!

The loss of our second baby occurred at a period of great
loss for the whole world—World War II, a time when we
parted with people and things most dear to us—hus-

bands, sons, doctors, sugar, tires, gasoline, shoes. For me it was a time of losing my husband to fight in a war just weeks after becoming pregnant.

This time the child was stillborn—a daughter. After all the tests said "dead," my mother would sit by me long hours, head cocked like a mother robin—watching, longing, hoping against hope for a flutter of life. Then came two days of unimaginably hard labor assisted only by student nurses—our regulars lost to the war. The coming of our family doctor to deliver that death, then his pacing outside my hospital room, wringing his hands in bewilderment. Why was his other new mother cursing and refusing her newborn while I, so eager to have mine, was wiping away tears—alone?

We had counted so heavily on that baby to fill the void, the aloneness, left when Chris' dad died so unexpectedly in his sleep following minor surgery just five weeks before. The new little grave dug next to his still fresh one turned Chris' second emergency leave into blackness and despair.

How God came in proportion to my need was amazing! Looking back, I realize there had been a deep, underlying assurance during those losses. Although at that young age I wasn't given to analyzing feelings and experiences, I remember the awful blackness being filled with an unusual presence. I recall vividly a special something, a quality in those bitter days of death that had not been there before. Nor after! It was just for that time. It was then that I had underlined Psalm 34:18 in my Bible: "The Lord is nigh unto them that are of a broken heart." I know now it was not a quality but a Person—God, coming in proportion to my need.

But God in His infinite wisdom knew that I had other needs in addition to being comforted with this enlarged proportion of Himself. He came in other, sometimes surprising and almost shocking ways during my aloneness through death. The number of different methods God used to produce gain for me is fascinating to explore.

Calling Me to Serve Others

With my first pregnancy loss, that miscarriage, God filled my aloneness in a way I certainly had not expected. How startled I was when our very wise pastor visited me, assured me of his understanding, and then promptly asked me to be the superintendent of our upcoming Daily Vacation Bible School. I blinked in disbelief. How could he even *think* of anything else when I had just lost part of my very life? (Six pregnancies later, I smiled at how I had just known there would never be another baby.)

But life really hadn't come to an end. God showed me another way He comes and fills voids—*by calling me to serve others.* While I poured my whole being into those 300 eager pupils for two exhausting weeks, I almost completely forgot my own loss. And I certainly was no longer alone. Yes, God had come in proportion to my need, when I didn't even know what my need was—filling the void by calling me to serve others.

Equipping Me to Teach Others

Another gain I discovered years later was that God had actually come in my need by preparing me for the privilege of teaching others—through these and subsequent baby-losses. Opportunities came in surprising and unexpected ways.

Back in the '60s when the problem of earth's exploding population was just beginning to surface, I was asked to speak at a Zero Population rally at our local Rockford College. After arm-waving speakers startled the students and members of the community, I found myself speaking on my assigned topic, "The Worth of a Human Soul." Wide-eyed, the audience hung onto every word as I explained the physical shock to my body at the involuntary aborting of a fetus and the psychological trauma of losing desperately wanted baby after baby. I had been invited to bring a "balance" to the rally, and I saw it happen. The crowd quietly dispersed, sorting out their thinking perhaps for the first, but certainly not for the last time. Another *gain* through my *loss*—the privilege of bringing another side of a controversial issue to those future leaders of our state.

Preparing Me to Counsel

How God came in proportion to my need and produced a most important *gain* because of the *loss* of my stillborn baby wasn't to be realized till years later. He knew my future need, and was preparing me for my role of listening to the heart cries of many young wives as a seminar leader.

In one of my prayer seminars, a young wife of a seminary student stubbornly refused to pray for God's will in her life. In her bitter anger toward God, she belligerently explained to me, "We prayed and prayed for a baby, and finally God answered and I became pregnant. He even gave us a name for our baby. Then three months later, right at Christmas, I lost it. I will never pray 'God's will' in my life again."

After much listening and comforting, I finally said, "Did you ever stop to think that the purpose of that baby's life was perfectly fulfilled? God's purpose—to bring you as a future pastor's wife to a place of complete and total surrender to His will—the absolutely essential ingredient for an effective ministry."

Wide-eyed, she pondered . . . understood . . . and literally crumpled before God. Then she prayed, "Only *Your* will in my whole life. Take all of me—for Your holy will." What a privilege I had *gained* because of my similar and equally shattering losses!

But I experienced another type of loss when one of our children died in infancy. A new kind of loss—aching, empty arms. But in this too, God came in proportion to my need. In addition to filling the awful void with His presence and undergirding arms of love, He came in the future tense—equipping me to meet the needs of others He knew I would be counseling.

After a "Lord, Change Me!" seminar in Canada this spring, a young mother in the autograph line, instead of handing me a book, said, "I want to talk to you. My little girl has just died." While she waited, I watched her struggle to keep the facial contortions of grief under control. After the last person left the line, she threw her arms around me and sobbed uncontrollably.

As I held her tightly and let her sorrow flow out in tears on my shoulder, I gently asked, "When did she die?"

"Last Sunday." Six days ago!

As our Judy's death at seven months flashed into my mind, I felt I should ask an all-important question. "Was your baby well?"

"No, she had brain damage."

Instead of giving her the standard Christian answer, "God was good to take her home," I took a completely different approach. For a moment I vividly recalled the sting when the wonderful doctor who delivered Judy said that to me at the time of her death. I had remained silent then, but my grieving heart was screaming, "A lot *he* knows about it! Sure, she was paralyzed from the waist down and couldn't ever walk. But he can't possibly understand that she's been the sunshine of our home, smiling and laughing with her eyes following every movement as I cheerily chatted at her." Of course the doctor was right, but in my grief, my brain hadn't been ready to sort out *that* fact yet. I knew that the one sobbing in my arms wasn't ready yet either.

So I said to her, "You know, I just have a feeling that God is going to use you to help other people who have children like your little girl."

Earlier that day she had participated in the seminar's exercise of reading the Bible *until* God speaks and then stopping and praying about what He said. (See *"Lord, Change Me!"* chapters 2 and 3 for complete coverage of this exercise.) The assignment had been Galatians 5:1 through 6:10, and I asked this young mother, "Where did God stop you in the Bible reading today?"

"Oh, He didn't say much," she mumbled and blew her nose. "Just Galatians 6:2."

"Hey," I beamed at her, "that's what He said, *'Bear ye one another's burdens.'"* Startled, she seemed almost shocked back into reality and the fact that there still was a tomorrow. "Now," I continued, "you just let God comfort you and heal you. Don't miss anything He wants to do for you *right now.* Then when someone comes to you who has just lost a child that wasn't normal, you can comfort her with all the comfort God has given to you—when He came in proportion to your need."

A feeble, relieved smile spread across her tear-stained face, and she hugged me again. This time not sagging in my arms in despair, but with the hope—and even a little flicker of confidence. I sent her on her way with 2 Corinthians 1:3-4 to cling to in the difficult days ahead:

Blessed be God . . . the God of all comfort; who comforteth us in all our tribulation, that we may be able to comfort them which are in any trouble, by the comfort wherewith we ourselves are comforted of God.

Gaining? Oh, yes. In her grieving *aloneness* experience God was equipping her too to fulfill the law of Christ. Now she would be able to understand and help bear other people's burdens in the future. In the same way, He had equipped me through those dark, stumbling days of death in the early years of my marriage—to meet the needs of others.

God Explaining Why

But all the ways God came in proportion to my need were not only for the future. Finally, during my third pregnancy-loss, God actually explained to me *right then* what my gain was through losing those three babies. At that time I had stayed in bed for 14 days with my feet elevated more than a foot, trying desperately not to lose again. But I did.

That wasn't to be the last death-loss for us, but it marked the time I began to see *how* God fills the void with Himself. God was starting to show me the gains He had planned for me. Things finally began to come into focus, a focus that was to continue throughout my life.

It was in my utter hopelessness that I cried out to God for His "why." And He answered—coming in a gigantic way in proportion to my gigantic need. He flashed before me "Romans 8:28," who He was—the God who was working out all those losses for my good. To those who love Him—to those who are called according to His purpose. (See *What Happens When Women Pray*, chapter 6, for complete story.) His *purpose*. But my *good*? Yes, it was God showing me that had those three babies lived, we could never have gone back to the college and seminary campus for seven years to be equipped for the life to which He had called us. Chris' dad was dead, leaving two children who were minors; and my own dad was an invalid. *His* purpose. And *my* good!

Joy
Understanding the "why" from God produced another gain—unbelievable joy. After those 14 days of living "upside down" in bed, the final verdict from the doctor came—dead. But this time God came in proportion to my need in a more personal way—just for me. He replaced the loss with *joy*.

I smiled inside at the eager young intern who, at seeing my joy, concluded he had uncovered a then illegal abortion right there in his hospital. His sleuthing intensified as he saw my doctor's name—the obstetrics teacher in that hospital! It was futile to try to explain during the intern's countless cross-examinations that God had turned my loss into joy. He didn't know, couldn't know, how God had come in proportion to my need.

After this "why" explanation from God, complete trust in Him started to come. It was then that His purposes for my whole life began to come into focus. I was gaining through my losses. Although I would not yet articulate that in those exact words until finding them in that poem several years later, it was then that *gaining through losing* took shape in me. Through the *loss* of an unborn baby's death.

Oh, how rich I am because God always took my death-losses and turned them into gains—for me and then for others!

Gaining through losing. It all came into focus the other day. The wife of the "little boy next door" from Rockford met me in front of the seminary where he is now an administrator. She had lost their expected baby in a miscarriage a few days before. I fought back the tears as she said to me, "God brought you into my life for such a day as this."

Has God come in proportion to your need?

6

To Die Is Gain?

To die is gain? The person is gone—forever. Everything that belonged to the deceased—money, property, family, life itself—all lost to him. But isn't it from our earthly perspective that we measure the losses of our loved ones? In our grief it is difficult for us to see that death is all gain for one who has died in the Lord. Paul wrote:

For to me to live is Christ, and to die is gain (Phil. 1:21).

This is our assurance, and we can cry with Paul, "O death, where is thy sting? O grave, where is thy victory?" (1 Cor. 15:55). My sister expressed it this way in a thank-you note for flowers sent for her saintly father-in-law's funeral: "Grandpa would have been 89 today. He can celebrate on a far higher plane than he could have with cake and candles!" If our loved ones have known Christ as Saviour and Lord, then we can have absolute assurance that for them all is gain. It is *our* sense of loss that makes us want them to stay here with us—not theirs.

But death *is* loss—crushing, numbing loss.

As we stopped into the mortuary right after my brother's death, Mother momentarily froze in her steps just inside the entry door. Gone! Then, bracing ourselves, we walked stoically into the room marked, "Mr. Luhman." As we stood by his casket, I took my frail little mother in my arms and, pressing my cheek against her white hair, whispered, "Mother, this is the ultimate Romans 8:28!" That had been our secret—ours through the years when life had crumbled and collapsed around us. When by earthly standards life wasn't worth living, we could always with a squeeze of the hand or an understanding glance whisper, "Romans 8:28." God working everything together for *our good*.

But that day this concept took on a new dimension— God working all things for *Bud's* good. Yet, somehow it was more than good. It was triumph! What was our *loss* was Bud's *gain*. Yes, we were gazing down at "to die is *gain*."

But my loss at my brother's death still jumps up at me in unexpected places—a plane stopover in Detroit, for instance. While Bud was living, every time a flight I was on made a stop in Detroit, I would get off, dash into the terminal and call him on the phone just inside the gates. The first time I came into that airport after he died, my feet dragged into the waiting room. A great void swept over my whole being. My stomach did a peculiar flip-flop as I shuddered inside. But it was my loss—not his!

Just last month while I was being driven to the Detroit airport following seminars, a vaguely familiar sight flashed past the car window. It was the fire department which housed the emergency squad Mother had summoned to try to resuscitate Bud. And there it was again. The loss welling up, unheralded, inside me. My loss—but not his!

Our Gain Through Their Gain

Our gain comes through knowing that it *is* gain for our loved one, not utter loss in an eternity without Christ. To have the assurance that our loved one has truly found

with Paul that "to die is gain" makes such a dramatic difference in our grief. It changes our despair to hope.

God gave this assurance in an unusual way to a young
woman grieving over the sudden death of her mother.
Knowing that her mother had attended a "Lord, Change
Me!" retreat (where we individually read His Word and
write God a letter about what He has said to us), the
daughter wrote in a letter to me:

> I found your "Lord, Change Me!" book in my
> mother's room when I was sorting out things
> after her sudden death in January. . . . And I
> found a letter she had written God at one of your
> retreats. I knew from reading it that she had ac-
> cepted Christ as her Saviour.

Her feeling of hopelessness had turned into confident
assurance.

Their Gain—Paradise with Jesus

During the loss of a loved one, we can start the process of
turning it into our gain by lifting our eyes, as our loved
ones do, to their gain—Jesus. Frequently, we hear of the
glorious experience of a Christian glimpsing heaven during the dying process. It happened to Stephen. He saw
Jesus—not only ready to receive him when he drew his
last breath, but also lifting him out of the misery of the
lethal stones that were snuffing out his earthly life.

> But he, being full of the Holy Ghost, looked up
> steadfastly into heaven, and saw the glory of
> God, and Jesus standing on the right hand of
> God. And said, "Behold, I see the heavens
> opened, and the Son of man standing on the
> right hand of God" (Acts 7:55-56).

Transcending the stoning, Stephen transfixed his eyes on
his Lord—Jesus—in heaven. Then there is recorded for us
one of the most remarkable conversations ever heard on
earth. Stephen, as he was being stoned, asked Jesus to
receive his spirit. His last words were addressed, not to

those humans around him, but to the Lord. Stephen knelt and cried with a loud voice, "Lord, lay not this sin to their charge" (7:60). Jesus was so real at the time of death that Stephen actually talked to Him.

To have communication with Jesus seems to be the privilege of many of God's children while they are dying. My stepfather told me that one morning his first wife, who was dying of breast cancer, told him that she would die that night—and she did. Her doctors and nurses had said, "She is not that close to death yet." But she knew that she was. Then he smiled as he reminisced: "Her face absolutely glowed that morning as she told me. And it glowed all that day." She had heard from her beckoning Lord, her Jesus!

How sad that some feel the dying one must be given drugs to provide a false euphoria or a dulling of the senses right out of reality. Depriving them of the right to die with dignity. Denying them the privilege, with the saints through the ages, of the experience of valiantly clinging to the greatest of all Comforters, the Lord Himself—"The Lord is my Shepherd; I shall not want. . . . Yea, though I walk through the valley of the shadow of death, I will fear no evil; for Thou art with me" (Ps. 23:1, 4). Pain relievers —yes. But the right to deprive the dying person of the privilege of being lifted, alert, into the arms of Jesus? Hardly.

And even our little Judy—just seven months old— seemed to sense Jesus' presence just before death. My husband was sitting by her hospital crib while she lay, unconscious, with her little fists tightly clenched. Suddenly, she opened her right hand, raised it upward as if reaching for something, held it there for a moment, dropped it—and died. Reaching for what—for whom? Jesus?

My heart thrilled again as my mother recently recounted how my dad, after being in a coma for several days, sat up in bed, raised his arms toward heaven, looked up and, smiling triumphantly, exclaimed, "Jesus!" Then he slumped back on his pillow in death.

Prepared

I had watched the price my mother paid for the privilege of knowing that my father was prepared to spend eternity with Jesus. For 25 years she had lived her Jesus before him, always in love and sacrificial giving of herself, never compromising—then came that moment when his doctor told him he was dying. After calling his denomination's pastor (whom he had never even met) to administer final communion, he said, "There's more to it than this, isn't there, Mother?"

"Do you really think so?" She once again repeated to him, "Just ask God to forgive all your sins, Daddy; and ask Jesus to come in as your Saviour." He did. Her Jesus became his Jesus!

Through the years my mother has paid the price for gaining the privilege of rejoicing in the certainty of the eternal destiny of many of her close relatives. Actively pursuing, loving, sacrificing, sharing Bible promises with them—until they too were ready. Her *loss*—their *gain*. With *their* Jesus!

As I was typing the manuscript for this chapter, the phone rang. It was someone calling long distance with a prayer request. "My boss' mother is dying of cancer. The doctors have given her two months to live. I just arrived to take care of her. She is angry with everybody—her children, the doctors, and me. Everybody. All I can feel is hate in her. Last night I even dreamed she was trying to poison me."

"She is reacting that way because she is afraid," I explained to her. "Afraid, because she knows she is going to die and is not ready. What she needs is your love and your Jesus. Share Jesus and His promises about heaven with her. Read John, chapter 14 ('In My Father's house are many mansions . . . ') to her."

"Oh," she exclaimed, "before I left home, her daughter said God had given her a Scripture portion for me to take to her mother. That's the Scripture—John 14!"

A completely changed lady called me a week later, "I did as you said—just shared my Jesus and loved her. And she just melted. She then wanted what I had. She accepted Jesus. Now she is a totally changed person— relaxed, joyful, not afraid to die." Prepared!

Many parents agonize for years over their children's readiness to meet God at death. For 30 years Mother had prayed every day for God to bring her boy back to Himself. The rest of us had prayed fervently too, though sometimes spasmodically. We interceded through all those years of his rebellion against God, and when he finally had said, "There is no God. I know there is no God!"

For two years Mother had prayed, "God, do anything You have to do to bring Bud back to Yourself." Then the accident. The car was traveling 50 mph and my brother, a pedestrian, was hit. Tubes, pumps, and intensive care were all that lay between him and eternity when our family arrived at the hospital. And Mother, almost collapsing, shuddered and sobbed, "Is it *my* fault—for praying that way to God?"

The next morning two of us could see him for ten minutes every two hours. Mother and I were first. I bent over his seemingly lifeless body and said slowly, deliberately, "Bud, . . . God . . . loves . . . you." The God he declared didn't exist! But at that moment there came the first flicker of life. Bud stirred. The minutes ticked by. I waited, fearing that any sudden shock would push him, unprepared, into eternity. But in desperation I knew I had to say something more.

"Bud . . . can . . . you . . . trust . . . Jesus . . . today?" I intoned. Suddenly he was awake, and through the tubes and hardware, he grinned at me and mouthed a strong, affirmative, "Uh, huh!"

God gave him over two more years to live, and it was

again Mother who took care of him when the doctors could do no more. In the last couple hours of his life here on earth, he reviewed for her his whole spiritual journey with God since he was a little boy—loving Him, leaving Him, denying Him, and then returning to Him. "I'll see you in heaven, Mother." With that he went to sleep. Just two hours later, with a violent lunge, he found himself in that heaven. Loss for her—but indescribable gain for him!

"Today shalt thou be with Me in paradise," promised Jesus (see Luke 23:43)—to the dying thief on that other cross—and to my brother. What a *gain* suddenly to be transported into heaven to be with Jesus, the very Son of God!

Gained—A Place

After the long years of questioning our brother's eternal destiny while he was alive, my sister still had a gnawing fear that perhaps Bud really hadn't known Christ as his Saviour when he died. When we met for the first time after his funeral, she asked, "If I could only *know for sure* where he is. Do you know for sure Evelyn? Has God told you?"

"Yes, I believe He has. It happened the first day I was home after Bud's funeral." And I told her exactly what I had scrawled in my notebook that morning.

Just before 5:30 A.M. woke with a start from a deep sleep. Looked out window. Cloudless sunrise! Shakily crawled out of bed and groped my way down to the dining room. It was alive with color. The sun radiating through the crystal chandelier at its peak.

As I stood in a mixture of trembly exhaustion and awe, I asked God to *recall* a Scripture. Searching my mind had produced nothing in that early morning stupor. *"In My Father's house are many mansions. If it were not so I would have told you!"*

My notes continued:

He knew my need. *Hope.* Not to look back to funeral, casket and cemetery, but *forward*, upward! *Bud.*

Then a sight I never had seen before. The sun kept striking the crystals and shooting blinding rays back into my eyes. Brilliant, all colors. Just a few, four or five at a time from the different crystals. Had I never stood exactly at that angle before? I don't know why, but *this morning was by far the greatest display of brilliant beauty ever.*

Then came, *"You believe* in God, believe also in Me!" *God!* The One who woke me out of a deep sleep at *exactly* the right minute. The One who recalled *exactly* what I needed to start living life normally again—*hope.*

Next my notes revealed my answer from God:

How could I *not believe* in the God who would do that? Happenstance? It would take a lot more "faith in happenstance" than I can muster this morning.

"I go to prepare a place for *you.* And if I go . . . I will come again and receive *you* unto Myself; that where *I* am, there *you* may be also!" Bud *was* prepared. He *is* preparing mine (my place) now.

Suddenly, praying was fantastic, *thrilling*—"I love You, Jesus." *Praise. Feeling* Him so real, tingly. Feeling God when I'm *alone.*

I can't wait to see all the gorgeous colors of the place God has prepared for us. Every foundation stone a different precious jewel with the glory of God lighting it and the Son of God the Light—intrinsic light, radiating through those jewels. A note in the margin of my Bible dated 4/16/74 (another time when the rising sun was in the right position to shine through my kitchen window and radiate through the crystals of the dining room chandelier) says, "Kurt, Dad, and I looking at spectrums on dining room ceiling. Read Revelation 21:18-23. What will heaven be like with, not the sun, but the glory of God shining through the precious foundation stones?"

Then I wondered how many more colors there are in addition to the visible rays of the spectrum we were viewing. New technology has already allowed us to see infrared and ultraviolet. How wide is God's heavenly color spectrum? After Bud's funeral I could see only the rays of the spectrum visible to the human eye. But what is Bud seeing?

Where All Losses Turn to Gains

How important it is for us to lift up our eyes to that place where all of the losses of earth turn to gains for the one entering eternity!

Angel Choir. My husband had a unique glimpse of this after he returned to his cadet training in the U.S. Air Force following his father's death. As Chris and his flight team were flying out over the Gulf of Mexico, someone had switched the dial from the radio range station to a regular broadcasting station to practice navigating by radio compass. Chris had hung his radio headphones up in the cockpit and leaned back, deep in thought about his father's recent death. Suddenly from those headphones, ethereal strains of music filled the cockpit:

> There's a land beyond the river,
> That we call the sweet forever,
> And we only reach that shore by faith's decree.
> One by one we'll gain the portals,
> There to dwell with the immortals,
> When they ring the golden bells for you and me.

In his mind Chris was standing in the midst of that great celestial angel choir in the presence of both his earthly and his heavenly Father. His emotions accelerated from awe, to joy, and then to hope!

Helen, a woman with whom I have prayed for eight years, recounted a similar experience. Her father, Dr. Henry Wingblade, to whom I was a secretary for four years when he was president of Bethel College and Seminary, was one of earth's spiritual giants. During his final illness, he was being cared for by Helen in her home. One day, while kneeling by his pain-wracked body singing hymns to him, she suddenly became aware of singing *with* an angel choir. And he was gone—to join that angelic host.

Whole. Chris and I were just reminiscing about our reactions to our Judy's death after she had lived seven months. From birth she had been paralyzed from the waist down. "The most important thing to me," he said, misty-eyed, "was that with a perfectly whole body she was running and jumping in heaven. No more handicap. Her life after only seven months here was perfectly complete with Jesus. She had accomplished on earth everything that God had purposed for her in that little deformed body. Judy standing—complete in Jesus."

"The fact that she was physically whole was the most important to me too, Chris," I recalled. In the days right after her death, I found myself imagining, almost fantasizing, that she was coming back down from heaven— healed. Sometimes coming into our home or sometimes with a dramatic descent into our church congregation as they gathered for worship—but always whole. However, gradually David's words after the death of his son by Bathsheba became a reality to me: "I shall go to him, but he shall not return to me" (2 Sam. 12:23). Heaven became so real to me I almost felt it was an addition we had built on our parsonage.

Reunion. Our children too have gained a special view of heaven as a real place because they have a sister there. Although only our oldest child Jan knew Judy, the two younger children, when they were small, always counted four children—including sister Judy. They knew there was a *place* and part of our family was waiting for us there.

The other day as I was sorting out a hoard of our son Kurt's favorite keepsakes for storage, I read for the first time what he, as a seven-year-old, had recorded on the "deaths" page of his Bible. He had not only included Judy, but had added an "Unknown Christenson" for our stillborn—who went to heaven 15 years before he was born. Another gain from a loss—a seven-year-old's thinking on death already in proper perspective.

As Chris watched our Judy die, his thoughts went to his dad and mine who would be meeting her for the first time. He saw our *enlarged family* forming in heaven. And when my brother died, I had an overwhelming sense of Daddy and Bud greeting each other. For years they had worked together in state highway construction. Then Bud was alone—so many years without his dad—until then. Gained—a family reunion!

Released—to Be with Jesus

Death is God's way of taking His own from this place of sin and sorrow and pain into His place of joy and peace and wholeness. So, since it is such tremendous gain for those who go to be with God, why is it so difficult for us to release them to Him? I think it's because the loss is ours. Because of the deep, devastating void it leaves in our lives. A grieving pastor whose wife had just died, wrung his hands in agony as he said to me, "Evelyn, we prayed and prayed and prayed, but she died anyway. She's gone."

Why are we horrified when we think we may have hastened the process by submitting to God's will, releasing them for His will? Doing so does not *cause* death. No, it just prepares *us* for the loss we will experience.

At a recent prayer seminar, we had prayed in the session just before lunch, giving God the most precious possession we owned—for His Will. The wife of the pastor of one of the largest and greatest churches of that area had prayed, "Lord, I've been holding back. I give you my whole family." It was a touching scene.

As we dismissed for lunch, a police car pulled up with the news that her husband had just had a severe heart attack. All I could do was mouth, "We'll pray," through the closed window of her car as it swept past me. Then, as we reconvened for the afternoon, the shock waves reverberated in the auditorium as we heard the announcement, "She didn't make it in time to see him before he died."

Had her releasing him to God *caused* his death? No. It was just God's way of preparing *her* for her loss in those next devastating hours.

A similar thing occurred when I revisited a federal penitentiary. The inmates shared with me what had happened to them through prayer since I had taught them to pray on my first visit. A female prisoner told us that at that time, she had released her most valuable human possession, her father, to God. Two weeks later she was informed by the prison administration that they had lost the official paper that should have informed her of her father's death and funeral. She decided to check through to see exactly when he had died. Horrified, she found it was two hours after she had released him to God. She burst into tears as she told us how the guilt of perhaps causing his death had haunted her all these months. "Did I kill him?" she cried.

"Was he a Christian?" I asked, trying to ascertain if death had been a gain for him.

"Yes, a fine one," she sobbed. Then I assured her that giving him to God had nothing to do with his dying. Her releasing him to God had prepared her for the shocking news of his death. Gain? In what way? By being prepared for the loss that was God's will—and her father's gain.

Why do we so tenaciously cling to the feeling that somehow it *has* to be better to stay here on earth? Paul struggled with the conflict of his willingness to stay here for the benefit of those he loved and his desire to be with Christ— which is far better. (See Phil. 1:22-23; 2 Cor. 5:8.)

A nurse in one of my Bible studies told me that her doctor-husband had obtained the best medical team available to operate on his elderly widowed mother whose leg needed to be amputated because of a circulation problem. After the surgery, the doctors huddled outside her room listening as she prayed and prayed—in Swedish. Frustrated at not being able to understand her, they asked, "What is she saying?"

"She's asking Jesus to take her home."

"She won't die," they all chimed at once. "The operation was a complete success. There's not a medical reason in the world for her to die." But she did. God had taken this saintly mother to be with Him—in that place of perfection and wholeness—and reunion with her husband. "For me . . . to die is *gain*."

We have a tradition at our house. The person celebrating a birthday or a special day is served breakfast in bed. The first Mother's Day after my brother's funeral, our son Kurt, getting up to cook my breakfast, found me at the phone downstairs in the family room.

"What do I have to do to keep you in bed so I can serve you your breakfast there?" he asked, feigning sternness.

But I had a reason for arising so early. "I'm calling Grandma, Honey. Uncle Bud died just one month ago, and this is her first Mother's Day without one of her children. There is a time change between here and there, and I wanted to get her early." I had visions of her being in deep despair and grief.

But I was amazed when she answered the phone. She cheerily said, "Hello," and seemed so on top of it all.

Apprehensively I asked, "How are you, Mother?"

Then she answered with, "What greater privilege could there be for a mother than to have one of her children in heaven on Mother's Day?" Yes, there continues to be that hurting void in her life. Yet it is always transcended by—where he is.

But I would not have you to be ignorant, brethren, concerning them which are asleep, that you

sorrow not, even as others who have no hope
(1 Thes. 4:13).

How good it is to watch the beautiful thing which is
happening at many Christian funerals these days—turning an almost pagan ritual of despair to a victory celebra-
tion for the one who has experienced final, glorious
gain—heaven. With Jesus, who, by His own death, se-
cured once and for all the fact that dying *can be gain.*

We were not created by God to die—to have our bodies
separated from our souls. This was the result of the fall in
the Garden of Eden. But God took away death's terror by
making death itself the doorway to heaven.

"O, death, where is thy sting? O grave, where is thy
victory? . . . But thanks be to God who giveth us the victory through our Lord Jesus Christ." For many years I
have asked my family to have the "Hallelujah Chorus"
from Handel's Messiah sung at my funeral. Turning their
loss into *gain* by lifting their eyes and hearts to the glorious
place of total and eternal joy—reigning with Jesus!

Culmination? No! Coronation!

Will your losses all turn
to gains—when you die?

7

Forsaken

Is separation by death the only cause of aloneness? Is there a *loss* of human association that can be even more difficult to bear than death?

In death there is generally the factor of God's sovereignty. We can find solace in the fact that the ultimate controlling force in death is God. Whether we accept it or blame Him, we still hide behind the knowledge that, after all, death is really beyond our control.

But not so when a loved one deliberately chooses to sever or replace a relationship. Forsaken! This can sometimes be a far more devastating loss than death.

Soon after my husband's father died, my mother-in-law and I shared a deep hurt with a mutual friend who had just learned that her husband had been unfaithful to her for several years. My heart ached as we watched her smile valiantly in public but writhe in agony at home as she struggled to swallow that bitter medicine.

When a loved one severs a relationship—especially when it leads to that final loss, divorce—the wound can be even deeper than death. It bleeds longer and festers. Whereas in death the departed one (if in Christ) gains, in divorce both lose. They lose the security, the oneness given them by God in marriage. Even in the mutual agreement to "part as friends," they both lose a stockpile of shared experiences, hopes, dreams, and possessions. And the innocent party (years of counseling heartbroken spouses have led me to believe there *are* some of those) not only suffers the same losses as the one who leaves, but frequently loses self-esteem, and goes on living in guilt and remorse. Guilt because of a sense of failure; remorse because things might have been done differently. Perhaps, just perhaps, the final break could have been avoided.

Gaining Through Losing?

What can possibly be *gained* in this kind of a ruptured relationship? This kind of *loss*? Except for those horrible cases in which anything would be better than suffering the physical or emotional battering and brutality at the hand of a spouse, is there any hope of coming through this kind of *losing* and actually *gaining*?

I have listened, astounded, as the forsaken ones have told me how God has met them at the point of their devastatingly deep needs. How He has taken over and filled the void with Himself. How they have been able not only to cope, but actually to find something given to them by God to replace the lost relationship.

This does not suggest that it is God's will that a marriage be broken. "What therefore God hath joined together let not man put asunder" (Mark 10:9). But God can pick up the pieces of the shattered life and put them together, so bound with His love, that the scar tissue is stronger than the natural flesh.

A beautiful, radiant, victorious woman came to me at a large Sunday School convention. After I'd taught the prayer lesson on the necessity of forgiving others, she told me an amazing story. She shared with me her struggles at trying to be a better wife in every way she could think of while her husband had been seeing a girlfriend for the past several years of their marriage. The other woman was even brazen enough to call and ask for her husband when she, the wife, answered the phone. Not wanting to give up the home-cooked meals, the laundry service, and the additional earnings his wife provided, he wanted to "have his cake and eat it too."

She told me of the three-stage progression through the years: first the bitterness, anger, and hurt; then the turning to God for advice and support; and finally experiencing *His* love replacing the human love she had lost. She said God had given her such a fantastic relationship with Himself that it was even better than the love she had *ever* known in marriage. Of course, God's *first* choice for her was not this loss of human love. But when, because of her spouse's rebellion against God's marriage plan, she was forsaken by her husband, God was there in proportion to her need. She said to me, "I've found Jesus absolutely sufficient. I still love my husband, but I have turned to Jesus and find all I need in Him. I can never begin to explain how much I love Jesus and how He fills and fulfills me."

I gave her a squeeze, then stepped back and gazed into that beaming face. "All I can see is Jesus radiating out of your beautiful face." It was true—that was all I could see.

Not Forsaken

How did this *gain* come about through her *loss*?

The answer is in this beautiful promise: "For He hath said, *'I will never leave thee, nor forsake thee'"* (Heb. 13:5).

This promise follows a rather startling series of brief statements of practical advice which includes: "Marriage is honorable . . . the bed undefiled . . . whoremongers and adulterers God will judge . . . be free from the love of money, being content with what you have." Then, *"For* He hath said, *'I* will never leave thee, nor forsake thee.'"* Interesting context for that promise.

This promise is a restatement of several pledges made in the Old Testament, one of which was the time-tested assurance Moses gave to Israel. How horrified, how alone the Israelites must have felt when Moses announced that after leading them from Egyptian bondage and through 40 difficult years of desert-wandering, he would not be going into the Promised Land with them. Forsaken by their leader!

But then Moses gave them the promise that proved to be true in that day, in New Testament times, and still today:

"Be strong and of a good courage, fear not, nor
be afraid of them; for the Lord thy God, He it is
that doth go with thee; *He will not fail thee, nor
forsake thee*" (Deut. 31:6).

After the similar promise is quoted in Hebrews 13:5, there follows one of the Bible's great "so thats"—"*so that* we may boldly say, 'The Lord is my Helper, I will not fear what man [people] shall do unto me'" (31:6). We can confidently know the source of our sustenance—the Lord. We don't have to be afraid of the possibility or reality of being forsaken by human beings. What worked for the Israelites works for us. Because of their example we can say with absolute confidence: "The Lord will never leave me nor forsake me."

Misplaced Expectations

Perhaps the reason so many are seeking alternative human companionship is because they have never found an adequate source to fulfill their needs. They may be expecting more than God intended from a human being. Should we expect anyone to be able to meet all of our needs at all times?

The daughter of a friend of mine recently had a discussion with a peer, at a Christian college in the South, who feels her husband is not meeting her needs. Summing up that conversation, her daughter said, "Mother, it is unrealistic that one person could meet another's needs for a whole lifetime."

"Yes, it is unrealistic. You are absolutely right," answered the mother. "No human being could do this. Only God can meet *all* our needs. *That is why we have God.* As we grow and change, our needs change in the same proportion, and we expect our mates to change and grow ahead of us and be able to meet our needs. But this is not possible.

"God does not *expect* any human to be able to do that and meet *all* of our needs *all* of the time. That is God's business. Today in marriage we are expecting a mate to do what *only* God is equipped to do. We are to live each day in the fullness of enjoying our mate, but never expecting him or her to be God."

Another wife said to me, "When my husband and I were first married, I had just found Christ and didn't fully understand what a Christian really was. I was dependent on my husband for all my needs, and he was just like God to me. Then I would criticize him because he didn't measure up to what I thought a Christian should be. My husband is head of our house, but he is not infallible. How much better it is to discover that we can't expect our husbands to be what only God can be."

Then she went on. "God is sufficient for every need that I *want* Him to be sufficient for. Sometimes we just *want* to feel sorry for ourselves, to nurse along the feeling that my mate 'doesn't understand my needs,' thus justifying the turning to forbidden ones. But God *is* sufficient for every need."

I too have found that not being understood, not having my needs fulfilled, involves a very difficult kind of loneliness, a sense of being forsaken. But in this *loss* I have found an overwhelming *gain*.

When a parent, a friend, a roommate, or a spouse cannot or will not meet my needs, it is really an advantage. For this has always driven me to the One who not only understands but cares. To the One who is always there to meet my needs. I have learned that a fantastic relationship with the Lord only develops in this kind of loneliness. What a privilege! The *loss* produces a *gain* that no human companionship could ever match. Fellowship with the Lord—who always understands. And bids us come to Him!

The Bidding One or Forbidden One?

Many people who are alone have told me about their beautiful, spiritual "love affair" with Jesus—being fulfilled in the pure and holy love of their Saviour. But all love affairs are not holy. It is possible in loneliness to turn not to the Bidding One, but to a forbidden one to find human companionship.

An attractive, unmarried 30-year-old Oriental woman confided to me at a seminar, "I'm in love with a man I can never have." Then hesitatingly she asked, "Will God really supply *all* my needs?"

"Yes, He will," I quickly answered, thinking she was referring to Philippians 4:19: "My God shall supply all your needs. . . ."

"No," she explained, "I mean *all* my needs," and suddenly I realized she was talking about her sexual needs.

Then I said, "To find sexual fulfillment from forbidden fruit is *never* God's way of meeting our needs. That is Satan's way. Ask God to forgive you and be done with that relationship."

I become weary of all those who, because they are deprived of a legitimate partner, defend to me their "right" to sexual gratification. I remember back in my college days there were two graduates who hadn't "landed their educated man" and decided that they had the *right* to sexual fulfillment. They pursued this life with two married men acquaintances.

Did the needs God supplies exclude those needs? Or didn't He even know they had a need? Jesus said that the

Father knows what we have need of before we ever ask Him (Matt. 6:8). So He knows our needs, and in Philippians 4:19 we are told that the *person* supplying them is God. And how many of them? All!

Of course, there are always those men who feel it is their "duty" to fulfill the needs of the lonely young girl, the wife whose husband is cold, the widow, the single adult, the divorcée. There are also women who feel it is the ultimate in kindness to give of themselves to the lonely young boy, the husband whose wife for a myriad of reasons is not available at the time, the widower, the divorced, or the never-married.

How does God supply *all* these needs? I vividly recall the indescribable loneliness I felt as a young wife, married just 11 months, when my husband was called into the service during World War II. My invalid dad would sit by the radio and keep track of the B-17 bombing raids in Europe announced on the daily news. No matter how recent a letter I had received from my pilot-husband, I always wondered whether I was a wife or a widow. I was never really sure till the day I sank weakly into a chair, clutching the cable that read, "Missions all done. Coming home. Love, Chris."

How I cringed in those war days at so many "alone ones" all around me who were seeking forbidden companionship—in the factories, in the bars, in the churches! Yes, the temptation and the opportunity were all around.

But I found that God would and did supply all *my* needs in that aching loneliness. The secret? He took away those needs and gave me complete satisfaction when I immersed myself in the Bidding One—Jesus. In His Word. In talking to Him. Receiving support, comfort, and guidance from Him. And immersing myself in serving the Bidding One—five times a week with the junior high schoolers of our church. And He was always there—loving me, occupying my time, controlling my emotions. Supplying *all* my needs.

But there is a forbidden one more terrifying than any human being. It is Satan, who goes about as a "roaring lion . . . seeking whom he may devour" (1 Peter 5:8). A college dean of women called me to counsel one of her freshmen, the daughter of a missionary couple on a continent where demon possession was common. Experiencing the loneliness of cultural and educational shock, this young girl had turned to fantasizing. "I'm having sexual intercourse with the Holy Spirit," she informed me.

"Oh, no, you aren't," I stated firmly. "You know, Satan is the deceiver. He counterfeits many pure and good things God has given us." The forbidden one! But for that lonely, forsaken college freshman, there was available the Bidding One—Jesus. "Come unto Me," He said to her. "I will never leave you nor forsake you. I will supply *all* your needs."

Innocent Victims—Forsaken

The greatest tragedy resulting from a broken home is its effect on the children. Forsaken! Whether the loss has been precipitated by deliberate separation on the part of the parents or by God through death, the children seem to suffer most—they experience the greatest loss. They understand least the trauma of separation. Often they experience *guilt:* "It was my fault that Mother and Daddy couldn't stay together. I caused it." Or *remorse*—wishing they had been better children so that a separation might not have occurred.

But children are sometimes faced with another problem when their parents are separated by divorce or death—they lose both parents. In some areas today, schoolteachers are being taught to handle children who have lost one‛ parent as though they had lost both parents—for many times they have. The parent left with the children changes, indeed must change, in order to cope and to assume the added role of the departed mate. That parent becomes a different individual with whom the children must become reacquainted. So the loss may be doubled.

A schoolteacher told me recently how much she appreciates her principal. When she could not seem to do anything with a little third-grade boy who lost his father just before Christmas, she asked her principal to talk with him. The boy came back to the classroom all smiles. Later she asked the principal, "What on earth did you do to him?"

"Well," he said, "I talked and talked and got nowhere. Then I took that little boy on my lap and told him I understood, because I too lost my father when I was a boy. And that little guy put his head on my shoulder and cried for 20 minutes."

I was reminded of Kum Ja, a beautiful little girl with an angelic voice who was a member of the Korean Orphan's Choir when they sang in our church several years ago. I can still see her splashing in our YMCA pool, relaxing, and having fun after a grueling concert tour. Today she is a citizen of the United States and is working on her doctorate degree in music.

Last summer she reminisced and shared with me some of her experiences as an orphan in Korea. With no one to care for her, she ate out of garbage cans and slept in doorways. You can imagine how startled I was when she said to me, "But I am one of the most privileged people in the world. With no human source of support, I had learned by the time I was two years of age, that God would take care of me. I came to know Him in a way few people ever have the chance to know Him. I am indeed a privileged person to have been deprived of all human relationships when just a little child, for I came to know Him in such a wonderful way."

Astounding? Yes. In her indescribable need, God had met that need in a way rarely experienced by most people. Abandoned? Certainly, although not intentionally by her deceased parents. But in her little mind—*forsaken*. Forsaken—until the God of the universe came in that fantastic way that almost defies human comprehension.

Jesus explained to His followers that He would not leave them *comfortless* when He left them (bodily) but would come to them (John 14:18). The meaning of the word *comfortless* in the original Greek surprised me: "forsaken and abandoned ones," "*orphans*"!

"I will come to them." He promised!

Children have a keen sense of being forsaken and abandoned when they are deprived of one or both parents. Do we lead them to the God who understands, fills the void, and supplies their needs? Have we given them the assurance that there is one Friend who will never, never leave them nor forsake them?

Nothing Can Separate

But there are other reasons for feeling forsaken in addition to death and broken homes. At times, security, acceptance, and fellowship are wrenched from us by our *own* actions or by the actions of *others*. And there are even times when separation is unavoidable. But no matter what the cause, the aloneness and sense of having been forsaken can be just as real and the need just as great as in death and in broken homes.

There is an assurance in the Bible for these times, too:
Who shall separate us from the love of Christ? Shall tribulation, or distress, or persecution, or famine, or nakedness, or peril, or sword? . . . Nay, in all these things we are more than conquerors through Him that loved us. For I am persuaded, that neither death, nor life, nor angels, nor principalities, nor powers, nor things present, nor things to come, nor height, nor depth, nor any other creature, shall be able to *separate us from the love of God,* which is in Christ Jesus, our Lord (Rom. 8:35, 37-39).

To be excluded, separated from one's peers as a high schooler, can be particularly painful. Kari Malcom, a daughter of missionary parents in China, told me of her feelings when she found herself in a Japanese concentration camp while still in high school. She had lost her father and all her material possessions, except what she could carry. "But my hardest loss came," she explained, "in a break with my close girlfriends with whom I had been through thick and thin. We daily met for prayer, asking God to take us out of that concentration camp. But God eventually convicted me of that prayer," she said, "and finally I could go to those meetings no more."

Her girlfriends became angry with her and ostracized her. She was excluded—emotionally and physically—forsaken by her close friends in a hostile, friendless environment—a concentration camp.

But Kari told me that the reason she had stopped asking God to release them from the concentration camp was that she had discovered a different prayer: "God, I will stay in prison the rest of my life *if I may only know You*." Yes, she had found a relationship deeper than one with a peer group. She had found a Friend closer than any of her earthly friends. Then she beamed at me and declared, "Since praying that prayer, all that matters is my relationship to God." Nothing could separate her from her God!

Jesus Understands
Jesus too must have known what it is like to be misunderstood and excluded from the close friends with whom He grew up and played as a child. His teenage group.

When He returned to Galilee with His fame spread through all the regions round about, Jesus found it to be quite different in His hometown, Nazareth. He stood up to read and preach in the synagogue, and His friends recognized Him only as a member of a local family, not as the Son of God. They "were filled with wrath, and rose up, and thrust Him out of the city, and led Him unto the brow of the hill whereon their [also His] city was built, that they might cast Him down headlong" (Luke 4:28-29). Jesus was more than emotionally ostracized by His childhood friends. He actually fled for His life as they violently forced Him toward a cliff so that they could push Him over to His death. His teen-age group!

This past summer I heard a prominent Russian pastor speak just two months after being released from a slave labor camp. He said, "I had to wear red stripes because I was considered the most dangerous kind of criminal in the camp. I was not allowed to fellowship with other prisoners. If the guards saw me talking to others, they would put us in separate barracks. Other prisoners were brainwashed against me as I was declared to be worse than a murderer."

But then he told us that no matter how segregated he was, he always had great fellowship with his Lord. His captors could not take that away from him! Separated— but not from God's love and companionship!

Jesus also understands what it is like to be ostracized by those in authority. Throughout His public ministry, there was a running battle between Jesus and the religious leaders of His day. They called Him a liar, attempted to stone Him, took counsel together to put Him to death, delivered Him to the civil authorities unjustly—until they finally cried to Pilate, "Crucify Him, crucify Him" (Matt. 27:22-23). Ostracized by religious leaders—but not separated from His Father's love.

A recent college grad poured out her heart to me for more than an hour. She said, "In college I had almost a 4.0 average and at graduation was given the highest scholastic honor my university bestows. I led the largest Christian organization on our campus for more than three years, my resumé is outstanding, and I'm going to be a high school teacher this fall." I sensed I was listening to a positive, deeply committed Christian.

"But," she went on, "I'm panicking. I'm going out into the world *alone*. I will be living in a little efficiency apartment—*alone*. I will no longer be a part of a group. I don't think I can handle it. All my friends from college are going their own ways or getting married." She had been sure that a certain young man was going to ask her to marry him. But instead at graduation time he said, "You are going to be happily married someday, but not to me!" Then he turned and left her—alone. Graduation—bringing not joy, but a horrifying sense of impending loss.

She told me she then prayed, "Dear Jesus, I'm afraid of being alone."

I asked her if all through her life and on that college campus there had ever been a time when God had not been with her in proportion to her needs. Thinking back for a few moments, she finally answered, "No, there has never been a time."

"Then," I continued, "there is no reason to think He isn't with you now, is there? God is always there to help in proportion to your need. If the need is great, He will be there in that proportion. When you are alone in that little efficiency apartment, look up at the ceiling and into the corners and know that God is filling every inch of that room. He *will be* there."

Tears welled up in her eyes. She threw her arms around me with a great big thank-you and good-bye hug all rolled into one, and stepped confidently out the door—into a waiting world. But not alone!

What had she gained in her frightening losses? She had learned that when feeling forsaken—even when the separations are unavoidable—that the panicking heart can be calmed with the assurance that God is there. Not alone! "Nothing can separate us from the love of God."

Singleness

Clinging to believing the promise that the Lord never leaves us is not always easy. Feeling forsaken by all those who might have, could have, or wanted to marry us can be difficult—especially when feeling forsaken *for* another—the one they did marry.

Does the Lord understand singleness? Did He feel that

kind of loneliness? Did He feel cheated? *Or,* because He was without a mate, did He experience His Father in heaven being with Him in a special way—as He glorified His Father and did His Father's will in all things?

A well-known Christian author and radio personality who has never married told me many years ago that she found singleness to be a blessing. She had discovered in her aloneness that she and God had a very special relationship. When she had said that, inside me a slight sneer raised its ugly head as I piously smiled and strained to agree with her. In my youthful inexperience, I thought she was only trying to justify her singleness.

Then I remarked a little smugly, *"I* have the best of *both* worlds. I have the privilege of having a husband *and* knowing God that way." But did I? Perhaps those of us who live in the security of mates who comfort, love, and provide necessities for us have never had the privilege of depending as completely on God—knowing Him to that depth. Had she merely become resigned to the state in which she found herself, *or* had she really found a relationship with God that only comes in aloneness? Since God understands our need for companionship—He created us that way—how natural and understandable that He will fill that need with Himself.

Jesus never married, yet at the end of His life He could say, "I am not alone, because the Father is with Me" (John 16:32).

Life's Separations
Life is full of separations for all of us. Times of feeling alone, abandoned, forsaken—unavoidable or deliberate. College . . . a new job . . . marriage . . . moving . . . a working spouse . . . hospital . . . nursing home . . . when we hit the bottom—or the top. These can bring anxiety, apprehension, and tension. They are real losses, and all need a solution.

This morning I witnessed a traditional family ritual out

by our curb. Little shoes were shined, hair freshly cut, new jeans still stiff, eyes shining—or were there tears? The last-minute clicking of the cameras ceased. The big yellow bus pulled away. Tears were blinked back. The first day of kindergarten!

As I watched, my mind whirled back over more than two decades of similar performances in our family—a series of separations in the pattern of our lives. The last one to flash on the screen of my mind was Kurt leaving for college. How similar it was to our first child going to kindergarten. I can still feel the depth of Chris' and my prayers that night for the boy whose newly vacated bedroom was next to ours. And our prayers for us. The empty-nest syndrome!

But again God showed me I was not alone. While reading the 15th chapter of John the next day, I wrote in the margin of my Bible, "Already feeling God's love when I'm alone. Kurt gone to Bethel last night." But then the note continued—another dimension—"I will be alone Monday night without Chris. Asked God to give me a great experience with Him." God answered my prayer then, and over and over again since—as He had done for so many years. Time-tested for over 35 years. Great experiences with God when I'm alone!

The year before, when Kurt left for college, I had spent much time alone with God because of my leg problem. My notebook bulged with recorded experiences with God— alone. When I returned home from the hospital after being in traction and was to stay in bed two weeks, my husband had to leave for the West Coast. At first a sense of aloneness swept over me like a flood. Kurt, popping in and out between college activities, worried aloud, "Mother, I should not leave you alone. But I have so much to do."

"Oh, Honey, I'm fine! I had the most wonderful day." And it was true. My notebook records that while praying alone that morning, I had felt an overwhelming love for God. I lay in bed—just reveling in His love, but mostly *my love for Him.* God had taught me years before that one of the definitions of *abiding* is "feeling My love when you are alone." Underlined right then in my Bible in purple ink were the words from John 16:32, "I am not alone—3/9/78." Jill Briscoe said this so well at a 1979 Bethel College Founder's Week service: "When your husband leaves and you are left alone, you can wallow in self-pity and drown *or* use the time positively. The greatest transactions take place when we are alone."

Our prayers when our children leave home are not only for them—but for ourselves. When either Chris or I must leave the other, we too have very special needs. While I was in Texas this summer, I sensed Chris was sad as we talked during our "good-night" phone call. Flashing through my mind was, *Oh, if only I could be there to comfort him.* I was torn between a strong impulse to just fly home to him and a desire to serve God there. But I could not leave, so I prayed to the One who would provide the comfort Chris needed: "Dear Father, only You can comfort him. Please, come in proportion to his need. You love him and comfort him the way I would if I could be there."

I first learned to pray this way for my husband at a time when he and I had flown as far as Colorado together. I stayed there for a seminar. The next day he was to fly on to California. As we knelt by our bed the night before he left, I became aware of a battle going on within Chris over leaving without me. He lingered in prayer, struggling with being separated from me—again. I prayed the prayer aloud for him then, but all through the night I kept praying silently, *O, Lord, You go with him. Surround him with Yourself. Lift him up. Give him joy. All the things that You can do.*

When I feel frustrated and helpless, sometimes a thousand or more miles away from Chris, what a privilege it is to know that not only am I not alone, but that he too is not alone. For my God is his God—who never forsakes him. From whom *nothing* can separate him.

But sometimes I am the one who travels alone. Unfamiliar airports, strange motels, stranger food, new faces. It is very lonely out there. As long as I am surrounded by the security of familiar places and loving people, I am not aware of needing God as much. But it is when I'm alone that my utter dependence on Him comes into focus. It is then that "I will never leave you nor forsake you" takes on real meaning. It is then that He really does come and meets all my needs—spiritual, mental, emotional, and physical.

I, with the Israelites of old, have the promise that has never failed—them or me: "I will never leave thee nor forsake thee."

Jesus Was Forsaken

Jesus understood being alone—forsaken. Toward the end of His ministry on earth, the huge crowds that wanted to make Him their king turned against Him—and followed Him no more. As He entered Jerusalem for the last time, they sang, "Hosanna in the highest" and instituted the first Palm Sunday by strewing palm branches at His feet. But by Thursday night, the forsaking had begun. His disciples, His closest friends, betrayed, denied, and forsook Him in His hour of great need. There were no familiar, friendly faces, no trusting supporters at His trial—not one!

But Jesus knew that He would be forsaken. He had already told them, "[You] shall leave Me alone." But He added, "Yet I am not alone, because the Father is with Me" (John 16:32). That fact is also true for all of us as followers of Jesus—we are never alone for the Father is with us.

But it was while suffering on His cross that Jesus had a sense of being forsaken that will never be experienced by any true follower of His. The Father was always with Him—until that excruciating moment when Jesus cried with a loud voice, "My God, My God, why hast Thou forsaken Me?" (Matt. 27:46). As Jesus hung on that cross, the Father had to turn from His Son in order that the Son could experience and bear our sins in His death.

That forsakenness will never be ours. We who deserve to be forsaken by the holy God will never be—because Jesus, who had never sinned, undeservedly bore that sin for us. We will never be forsaken as Jesus was—for us.

Don't Waste Your Forsakenness

Forsakenness comes in degrees—from the shattering of death or divorce to the first day of kindergarten. But don't waste one of them! Practice experiencing all of God's unchanging steadfastness in the little bumps and in the enormous disasters so that, no matter what kind of forsakenness engulfs you, you can experience what Paul did. Join him in his absolute assurance, born experientially out of every conceivable loss, through temporal adversities and spiritual conflicts, summing up with almost ecstatic confidence: "[Nothing] shall be able to separate us from the love of God, which is in Christ Jesus our Lord" (Rom. 8:39).

Confidence *gained* through our *losses!*

One evening this past summer, Chris, his sister Shirley, and I were hiking along the shore of Lake Michigan. We were exhilarated and chatting happily when suddenly my weak leg started to drag, making marks in the sand. There was only one thing for me to do—turn back. I felt a twinge of forsakenness as I turned to walk to the cottage—alone. But as I saw only the lake and the sand stretching out in front of me—no other person in sight—my heart suddenly leaped within me. "I love You, God. Just You, God. What a great feeling. All alone with *You.*"

I recalled how I felt just before Chris and I were married, when there were places it was not proper to be alone with Chris. And that insatiable thirst to be alone with him. "This thirst is how I feel about You, God."

I hiked, my heart soaring. Then I sat on the sand, just so

the lapping waves missed my feet, and watched the pro-gressing sunset. I hugged my knees. A thrill tingled down my spine. Not forsaken! Not alone! God!

Don't waste your losses!

8

Losing My Right to Run My Own Life

No matter how important the loved one whom I have lost in separation or death may have been to me, there is one other human possession who always wants to be Number One—the one I cling to most dearly and struggle so hard to keep; that being who is called by my name—myself. It is the "I" in my life, the "I" that I strive the hardest to protect and nourish.

Even in dealing with losses by death, I have clung to this prized possession—protecting, pampering, and preserving this "I." At times it becomes very difficult to give up the "rights" of this prized possession of mine. The rights I feel are legally, rightfully mine.

How like William Ernest Henley we are in forcefully asserting, if not aloud to others, at least in the secret recesses of our hearts the words of his *Invictus*:

It matters not how straight the gate
How charged with punishments the scroll,
I am the master of my fate;
I am the captain of my soul.
(Arthur Quiller-Couch, ed., *The Oxford Book of English Verse*, Oxford University Press.)

We feel we have the right to sovereignty over our own lives. But do we? Is this, or has it ever been, the *right* of the Christian? Is it the difference between knowing Christ only as Saviour or as both Saviour and Lord?

Thomas, on seeing the wounds in the risen Saviour's hands, immediately enjoined the disciples' familiar name for Jesus, "Lord," with the absolute title of deity: "My Lord *and* my God." After that there is no record of that Greek word *kurios* ever being used by believers in addressing any but God and the Lord Jesus. It was a term they used interchangeably with God—and Jesus. (See William E. Vines' *Expository Dictionary of New Testament Words*, Revell, Volume III, p. 17.) Sovereignty—not I but Jesus.

Peter, after the resurrection and ascension of Jesus, told those who had crucified Him that God had made Jesus *both* Lord and Christ (Acts 2:36). It was because of that resurrection, he explained, that the full significance of the title *Lord* could be understood. Lord—having power and authority. Also we as believers have been translated by God "into the *kingdom* of His dear Son" at redemption (see Col. 1:13-14). Jesus spoke of His sovereignty in Matthew 15:24, "If any man will come after Me, let him *deny* himself."

The Handmaid

From my teens on I have consciously worked at allowing God to be sovereign in my life. At every prayer seminar that I teach, I personally re-pray my commitment along with the others as we bring ourselves into total conformity to the will of God.

I always thought I had submitted completely to God's will. But in the fall of 1977 at a retreat in Indiana, God gave me a word that solved the whole problem of sovereignty for me: *handmaid*. While I sat on my bed with two friends at that retreat, studying Peter's explanation of Pentecost in Acts 2:14-18, the word *handmaidens* in verse 18 just seemed to jump off the page at me. The letters momentarily appeared to be eight inches high and half-an-inch thick. God was saying "handmaid" to me.

With that impact I struggled in prayer trying to submit absolutely to God. He was suddenly pointing out the two areas of my life I just *thought* I had surrendered to Him. Then in a flood of tears, I bowed before Him till my head touched the mattress—in complete, total submission. "Lord, I want to be Your handmaiden."

Flashing across my mind came Mary's response to the Angel Gabriel at the Annunciation: "Behold, the *handmaid* of the Lord; be it unto me according to Thy word" (Luke 1:38). Mary responded immediately after he told her she was to be the mother of the coming Saviour. I couldn't wait to get home to my reference books to see if *my* word was the same in the original as the one word Mary had used. Had I said to God what Mary had said? Elated, I discovered—yes, I had! Then I looked up the definition of the word *handmaid* in many reference books. In Mary's day it meant the lowest term in the scale of servanthood— "one who gives up her will to do the will of another." Sovereignty!

Tucking the exciting discovery into my heart, I went to bed, but lay awake, pondering in the night what Mary had been willing to give up, to *lose*, in order to be the handmaid of the Lord. What losses would result from making God, not herself, sovereign?

Mary was a Jewess who knew that according to the law she could *lose her life* by stoning if found to be pregnant out of wedlock. Still she was willing to allow God's will to be accomplished in her body. Willing to live contrary to the expectations of the existing religion of her day. Willing to *lose her reputation*—a most precious human possession. Willing to endure the suspicions and whispers and peering eyes of the neighbors in that little town of about 15,000 persons. Willing to *hurt Joseph*, the love of her life, when he learned she was pregnant by another. Willing even to risk *losing her beloved* and giving up all the plans for her future with him, knowing that legally he could give her a private writ of divorcement or divorce her in a public scandal. Mary—willing for God's will. But probably she was hoping she wouldn't have to change her lifestyle, dreams, and priorities—but willing!

I gulped, "Lord, did I really say *that*?"

Later, when I took inventory to see if I really was willing to apply what God had said to me at that retreat, I found myself struggling. It was easy to pray, "I want to be Your handmaid, Lord," But was I actually willing to *become* the handmaid now that I understood what it really meant? What would be the losses in my life?

The big possibility loomed—the love of my life—Chris. What if God would want him? Could I be willing? Or even willing to hurt him? On the morning of Chris' next birthday I found myself praying for him—and then for me. Struggling with the thought that *if* this was the year of his life that God would call him, was I willing? That wrestling with God took a couple hours before I could honestly say, "Lord, You are sovereign."

Was I willing to lose *my* reputation? This spring I reported on *that one* to my Advisory Board, citing three almost simultaneous examples. First, phone calls from a large Canadian city had me stumped. The reservations for my upcoming seminar had suddenly stopped cold. They had poured in for a while, then nothing. Checking, we discovered that a Christian leader in that city had spread some rumors with this question: "How does that Evelyn Christenson have the nerve to come up here to teach us to pray when she and her husband are in the middle of a divorce?" Convincing them that Chris and I had never been happier turned the tide (and my hurt pride). The seminar was filled—with several hundred turned away.

Then I told my board that next my publisher was frantically trying to locate me. When he did, he said, "Call Australia immediately. Your speaking tour there is being questioned." After much probing and questioning . . .

"Have you ever?" . . . "Did you and your husband . . . ?" the trans-oceanic call ended in hearty peals of laughter. We decided that the information "from a very reliable source" had really been lies. Halfway around the world. Rumors really do fly!

Lastly, I reported to my board that at a recent retreat, after four of the five days had lapsed, one of the administrators confessed over pizza that she had been assigned to keep an eye on me to see if I really was doing so-and-so, and if I had sort of flipped since last being with them and was now carrying on like a mad woman. Someone had warned them that it had happened to me just two weeks after our last retreat. My question, "And did you *see* me acting like a mad woman?" released gales of laughter and then a great big, affirming hug.

Our treasurer had listened intently as I verbally licked my wounds, then asked a question that was a good reminder for me, "Haven't you been praying to lose your life for Christ's sake, Evelyn? Well, what is more you, your life, than your reputation? That's *you!*" Yes, the human possession I'm most fearful of losing is *me*.

And I too had to admit I wouldn't be overly anxious for my friends to peer out at me and say, "Tut, tut. Look what that Evelyn is up to now." And being misunderstood by *my* status quo church or Christian friends? Being God's handmaid involved more *losses* than I had counted on. The magnitude of what I had prayed overwhelmed me.

The Handmaid's Gains

But were there no *gains* through Mary's *losses* in becoming God's handmaid? Oh, yes, they were legion. What awe must have swept over her when she realized that from among all the Jewish virgins through the centuries, *she* had been chosen to be the mother of the Son of God— bursting forth in her Magnificat that "henceforth all generations should call her blessed" (see Luke 1:46-55).

What a thrill to have the familiar prophecies about the

coming Messiah fulfilled in her! What a privilege to actually be the one chosen to experience Isaiah's prophecy concerning "Immanuel," "God with us" (see Isa. 7:14)—inside her own body! What sensations of ecstasy must have welled up, unheralded, in her whole being when she realized the little one kicking in her body was in reality the very Son of God.

While in labor in the town of Bethlehem, how overwhelmed Mary must have been as she recognized God's timing in placing her, because of the taxation, in just the right city. Micah was right. Bethlehem! The rest of that prophecy was being fulfilled—"Ruler in Israel; whose goings forth have been from of old, from everlasting" (Micah 5:2)—being born right then from her very body. A preexistent Deity!

What kind of anticipation must have been Mary's as she gazed down into that newborn's face—knowing that this was the One who would save His people from their sins? What did she ponder in her heart when the arriving shepherds told of hearing the announcement of His birth by a host of angels over their fields near Bethlehem? "A Saviour—who is Christ the Lord!"

What joyous reverence must have swept over her when later the wise men found Him after following a star in the East until it stood over where the young Child was. They fell down and worshiped Him—knowing that He was the King of the Jews. How dazzling for a poor, humble Jewish girl to see all of that wealth—for Him—her offspring!

Perhaps the most mind-boggling gain for Mary was that God used her own body to produce her own Redeemer! He was coming to save His people, of whom she was one, from their sins. Then, some 30 years later, after the agonizing sorrow of watching her son being crucified for all our sins—to be given the unutterable joy of seeing Him after He had risen from the dead. Her Saviour. Having paid the price of sin once and for all.

Then Mary was in the Upper Room with the 120, hearing the apostles, flushed and glowing with excitement, reporting that they had seen her Son ascend to His Father in heaven in the clouds. Gains? Unspeakable! But all because she was willing to *lose* the sovereignty of her self and become God's handmaid.

The Missed Promise

Were there to be *gains* for Evelyn too for having prayed that prayer? Using Mary's word *handmaid* just before falling asleep that first night home from Indiana? In the middle of that night, as I sleepily groped my way to our bathroom, six more words from Acts 2:18 flashed into my mind: *"I will pour out . . . My Spirit."* A light burst upon my thinking. I had been concentrating so hard on being the handmaid, *I had missed the promise!* It was Joel's promise that we had been reading in Acts 2, the promise which Peter said was being fulfilled before their very eyes. God's Holy Spirit would be poured out—on His servants and His handmaidens (see Joel 2:29).

Back in bed I saw it all come into focus. Was the Annunciation the only time the Holy Spirit had been poured out on Mary? Oh, no. She was listed among those 120 gathered in the Upper Room for prayer (See Acts 1:14), on whom this part of the prophecy was being fulfilled. She had experienced the other prophecies being fulfilled in her—enough to produce the actual Son of God in her body. But was she expecting to be *one* of *these* handmaidens? This is the last *gain* recorded for Mary in the Scriptures. Her other handmaid-experience had been so singular; in a way, no other person ever had or ever will be a handmaiden in that sense.

I wondered how those 120 were praying between the Ascension and Pentecost. The apostles; the women; Mary, the mother of Jesus; and His half brothers. Were they praying about their desire to be only *His* bondservants and handmaidens—and thus having the prophecy fulfilled in them? Was Mary reviewing her submission to God's will that she prayed for more than 33 years before? Were the brothers of Jesus claiming their elder brother as *their* Lord—expressing their desire to be His bondservants? Were the apostles who had deserted Jesus and even denied Him—and then had seen Him ascend to His Father in glory—were they submitting to be His bondservants? Were the women who traveled with Jesus, who supported Him with their funds, and who were the first to see His resurrected glory, praying this prayer? His bondslaves! His handmaidens!

Lying there in bed I suddenly saw it—for me. On those who completely submit to Him, *He pours out His Spirit.* Understanding this concept explained why at that retreat the very next morning God had poured out His Spirit on those over a thousand women—as they confessed their sins aloud in prayer, wiping away their tears of repentance. "The only thing wrong with this retreat," they complained, "is that you forgot to tell us to bring our boxes of Kleenex."

We had experienced the *Holy Spirit in His rebuking and reproving role!* It explained why a couple hundred of them who followed me to my next prayer seminar just exploded with excitement over God's response to their retreat praying—it had changed them, their husbands, relationships within families and their pastors. Again the *Holy Spirit— healing, reconciling!*

At that seminar the Holy Spirit reproving *the world* of sin (see John 16:8-9) came into focus as two bewildered young women stood before me. As we entered a vacant Sunday School room, they blurted out, "We don't know if we really have Jesus as our Saviour." I questioned if they had ever asked Him to come in as their Saviour.

"I did when I was a little girl, and I feel as if I'm slapping Jesus' face to ask Him in again today," one answered.

"I don't think I ever did," said the other.

Then I explained that if they weren't sure, Jesus would understand and wouldn't be hurt. They could pray that prayer just in case they hadn't meant it before, if they wanted Him now. They both started to cry, and I put one arm around each of them and held them close. As their tears formed wet spots on my shoulders, two young women made sure of their eternal destiny that noon. *The Holy Spirit wooing!*

I see it now, God's promise given through Joel that the Holy Spirit would be poured out—with His convicting, wooing, empowering—on and through those who were totally submitted to God. His *bondservants*, His *handmaidens*. I had struggled so hard with the submission that I'd missed the promise! I had experienced the promise without recognizing it for what it was.

The Bondslave

While studying the word *handmaid*, I discovered that it was the feminine equivalent of the masculine word, *bondslave*. Some of those men praying in the Upper Room before Pentecost described themselves as bondslaves in their epistles in the New Testament. Peter, who betrayed His Lord, used it of himself in introducing his second letter. Even Jesus' half brothers, James and Jude, opened their respective books referring to themselves as bondslaves of Jesus Christ. It was a favorite description of Paul for himself. Bondslave—the one (this time a male) who gives up his will to the will of another.

But what about the man in Mary's life? Did God choose a bondslave to be the husband of His handmaid? Although there is no record in Scripture that Joseph called himself a bondslave, I noted as I studied his life that his actions and attitudes proved him to be one of God's greatest. When the angel came to him explaining that Mary was pregnant by the Holy Spirit and would bring forth a Son who would save His people from their sins, Joseph's immediate response was to rise up . . . and take his wife. No questions. No hesitation. Just instant obedience.

Then I questioned—what "rights" did Joseph surrender, lose, in order that God's will be done? Joseph gave up the right to be *included in the Annunciation.* Spontaneous acceptance of God's exclusion of him from the most important announcement on Planet Earth up to that time—the Messiah was coming! I've often wondered how Joseph felt when Mary, not he, found favor with God and when the angel came only to Mary—not to both of them together. There is no indication that he submitted grudgingly or angrily—only that he complied completely with God's wishes for his espoused wife's life.

Joseph also gave up the right to *clear his name* of fathering a baby before marriage, which he could have done by giving Mary a writ of divorcement. That really took a big man! And he gave up the right to his *feelings of embarrassment* at taking a ready-to-deliver *espoused* wife to be taxed with him when legally they had no right as yet to have come together (see Luke 2:5). How my heart ached for him.

Also, Joseph gave up the right to marry a maiden who wasn't pregnant. The right to father the first child of his bride. My opinion of Joseph was growing by leaps and bounds.

But Joseph became the most beautiful example of a bondslave when he gave up the rights of a bridegroom. He put aside all his human needs and wants and lived a life of self-denial. He kept his bride a virgin through their honeymoon and their marriage till her baby was born—so that God's prophecy in Isaiah could be fulfilled.

When Joseph unhesitatingly obeyed the angel's message, he knew that he had given up the Jewish father's right to name the baby (for God had already named Him—see Matt. 1:21). He also gave up the father's right to direct his child into his life's work (God had already planned His life).

My discoveries of what Joseph had given up, his *losses,* continued after the baby Jesus was born. He was God's bondslave to the extent that he gave up the right to go home to his honeymoon cottage in Nazareth after the birth of Jesus. Rather, he was forced to flee from Bethlehem to Egypt in order to save Mary's (and God's) Son from the wrath of King Herod. Then he had to spend the first two years of their marriage in a foreign country among strangers.

Although Joseph may not have known it, he gave up the right to have the lineage recorded in his name as was the prerogative. He received no credit in the Holy Spirit-inspired genealogy in the Gospel of Matthew. The wording changed from the long line of "begats" to the feminine singular, "Mary, of whom . . ." Confirming Mary's virginity—yet excluding Joseph with divine finality.

I concluded we have not given Joseph enough credit. What a specimen of manhood—a newlywed bondslave of God. I saw Joseph as one of the most powerful examples in recorded history of a man who was willing to give up his will—physical fulfillment, reputation, and personal plans—to the will of God. Bondslave!

The Bondslave's Gains

But was it all *loss* for Joseph? Oh, no. Because he was willing to give up his rights, he won staggering *gains*. I eagerly tallied his rewards.

First, Joseph was chosen by God to be the head of the home into which God was entrusting His only begotten Son. God was giving Joseph the privilege, according to Jewish custom, of *training* one of the preexistent members of the Godhead—the Son—through His formative years on earth. And what overwhelming waves of awe must have swept over him from time to time as he looked at the little boy learning at his feet—knowing He was destined to save His people from their sins.

What a privilege for Joseph to be entrusted by God with the *preservation* of the Saviour of the world—before, during, and after His birth. How carefully Joseph must have protected that unborn fetus; how seriously he must have taken his responsibility of aiding in the birth of the very Son of God. How Joseph must have tingled as God confirmed His confidence in him, telling him in a dream to flee to Egypt to preserve the world's Saviour.

Another gain for Joseph was that he was given the fulfillment of *providing all the human needs* of the very Son of God while he was growing up—food, clothing, shelter, security. That incentive must have lifted the weariness during those long hours in his carpenter's shop.

How Joseph must have reveled in the fact that both he and God had picked the same maiden—he, for his wife; God, for the mother of His Son. The woman God had chosen to be the most blessed among all women! *Gains* inexplicable!

The Marriage Triangle

I believe there was one more gain for Joseph and Mary, when together they submitted their wills to the will of Another. God did not break up their love affair, but most likely gave them the best marriage imaginable.

A third human invading the marriage relationship always spells disaster. Hurts, suspicions, lost trust, broke homes, forsaken families, disturbed children—all results of the third party intruding where he has no right to be.

But there is One whose presence creates just the opposite effect when He is asked to be included in a marriage. This One expects submission, obedience, loyalty, and love which, instead of disrupting a marriage, enhance it. Instead of dividing the marriage, becomes its cohesive force.

The only third Person capable of doing that for a marriage is God Himself! Instead of forcing a wedge between the couple, God draws them together. Inviting God's will into a marriage unites them until, side by side, they are so close it is hard to distinguish that there are two people forming the triangle, with God at the apex.

And so it was with Joseph and Mary. The perfect example of God's sovereignty—two separate lives—in unspeakable joy becoming one in Him. A bondslave and a handmaid—married! Both being willing to give up their own rights to obey God's will. What perfect material for the creation of a perfect marriage!

Who's Number One?

Without my knowing it, God was preparing me this summer for a showdown decision. At a convention attended by several thousand, I had felt a great moving of God during our prayertime. The next morning as I prayed for that day's meetings, I asked God to send a great revival to that conference—at the grass roots level. Then I asked Him, if it was His will, to allow me to be an instrument in it.

"O God," I corrected, "not an instrument. Organs are great musical instruments, and many times I have heard them praised for what *they* are. Make me only one of the *empty pipes* through which *You* pour Yourself in glorious music—powerfully moving the people."

Returning home I went to a physiatrist for some leg exercises and he routinely took my blood pressure. His stern eyes never left mine as he said, "Your leg is only the oil stick of your whole physical condition. Your blood pressure has skyrocketed. You may have two days to live— maybe two months—maybe two years. In fact, you may not get home from this office in your car. You'll have to stop trying to hold the whole world in your arms. You'll have to change your lifestyle and take time for Evelyn— *every* day. You're going to have to start looking out for Number One."

Numbly I drove home, sorting out the priorities in my life, reviewing my standing commitment to God—wanting only His will, whatever that might be, all my life. Should "I" become Number One in my life? I struggled in prayer, but by the time I went to bed I had settled it—once for all. Reaffirming my lifelong desire, I prayed, "Lord, *You*, not Evelyn are Number One in my life. It doesn't matter for how long. I am Your servant, Your handmaid."

During my following retreat at Mount Hermon, Calif. unbelievable problems were being shared with me. I found myself holding those women one by one in my arms, weeping with them, praying for them till past midnight. After sleeping three hours that Saturday night, I was wide awake pleading with God. "Lord, I want to hold every one of these hurting women in my arms. Every one."

As I lay there in unbroken communion with God, I was offering, not actions, but my whole self to God—to be expendable for Him. Then a burden started to come from Him. I felt that commitment growing and growing inside me till I could see—not Mount Hermon, not the state of California—but the whole world.

"Lord," I cried, "let me hold the *whole hurting world* in my arms!"

What happened the next week was just a sample of the fantastic joys, open doors, and gains that God was planning for me. To minister around the world!

The phone started ringing. "When can you be in Hong Kong for a seminar?" . . . "Trans World Radio in Guam just finished playing both sets of your tapes—to one fifth of the globe." . . . "Kathy leaving for round the world. Will check on the Japanese translation of your book and your trip to Japan while there." . . . "Transoceanic call firmed up Australia and New Zealand itinerary." . . . "Friends from San Diego want books and tapes. . . . Leaving for Singapore in two weeks to teach prayer." . . . "Publisher's meeting—England and South Africa must be next," they said. I was reeling.

I put my head on my kitchen table and sobbed, "Lord I'm not worthy!" No, I'm not. And neither was Mary—or Joseph. But it is on His handmaids and bondslaves, those who are willing to give up their wills to the will of Another, that God pours out His Spirit!

Perhaps the concept of *gaining* through *losing* my rights to myself is best summed up in a Christmas present from our daughter, Jan, last year. The previous summer she had painstakingly transcribed for me on the typewriter, word for word, the tape recordings of the actual prayer seminar from which I produced the book, *What Happens When Women Pray*.

The letter accompanying the Christmas present said:
Dear Mom,

It's almost hard for me to give this present be- cause it's like giving a piece of myself away. It's letting you peek inside me for just a minute. I wrote this poem for and about you while I was typing your manuscript several summers ago. I want you to have it, not because it's good, but because it's me. And it's you. And it's the min- gling of us both. So here I am—like your little blonde-braided girl again, holding out a bunch of dandelions to you—just because I love you. With love brimming out my eyes—Merry Christmas to the most wonderful Mommy in the world. . . .
Your Janny,

Her personally hand-painted, beautifully framed Christmas present said:

Let go
Unclench
So you can hold
The wonders of His will
Exchange your finite
for His infinite.

Who's number one in your life?

9

Losing My Right to Harbor an Unforgiving Spirit

Have you ever battled with your right to harbor an unforgiving spirit? When you are hurt by what someone says or does, do you feel you have the "right" to turn that person off, shun him, or even hate him? When things just aren't the way they used to be, do you feel you have the "right" to keep it that way?

I have been teaching the biblical precepts of forgiveness from my book *What Happens When Women Pray* for several years now. I used to wonder how effective this teaching was—if the actual forgiving really worked.

But I don't wonder anymore. One of my greatest joys has been watching these instructions bring visible results in the lives of those doing the forgiving. I have been astounded at the *gains* that have come to those who have been deeply hurt and then, by forgiving, have indicated their willingness to give up, *lose* their "right" to nurse a wounded spirit.

Many have said I should write a sequel to that first book. So here it is—at least in part, telling what happens to those who have forgiven someone as they have prayed. I have used many of these illustrations in subsequent prayer seminars, but now here they are for you who are reading this book. Some of the *gains* I have observed:

Transformed Lives

Watching the changes take place right before my eyes as hundreds of thousands have forgiven someone right in our seminars has been enlightening to me. Each time the participants pray aloud in their little groups of four, I stand amazed as burdens which have been carried for years are lifted, as people are set free from debilitating attitudes. I see them enfold weeping prayer partners in their arms, and I catch the surprised expressions of indescribable joy spreading across faces as they are released from feelings of hatred and bitterness. And then watch the hugs of reconciliation.

So many participants as they stop to say good-bye, beam, squeeze my hand and say, "You'll never guess what happened to me today." And then their story—victory! Or some will press a note in my hand telling me of the depth of the hurt and then the height of the relief as they forgave that day.

I have been inundated with letters from people who have read the chapter on forgiveness in *What Happens When Women Pray,* and have bowed in prayer—applying the scriptural teachings—with such fantastic results. I have met strangers who are just exploding with the life-changing results because they applied those simple principles and took the step of forgiving. The *gains* for the ones doing the forgiving have been astronomical!

Arriving at a large southern prison to teach the principles of prayer, I was stopped by a tall blond male inmate with a fine athletic build. "I just must talk to you—alone. I have to tell you what your book did for me." To find a place to be alone in a prison is difficult, but we were told we could sit in a corner of a heavily trafficked hallway to talk.

"Evelyn, I have been a Christian since I was a little boy,

played football at a large Christian university, then earned my first million dollars playing professionally. After I was injured and could no longer play, I squandered my million trying to keep up the lifestyle I'd learned to love. When the money ran out, I panicked and turned to organized crime. I ended up on the FBI's 'Ten Most Wanted List,' was eventually caught, and drew a 240-year-consecutive sentence.

"I have a delicate wife whom I love dearly. I protected her so well when I was on the outside that I never let her even carry a bag of groceries. But since I've been in here, she has had to hold down two jobs to support our four children. It just breaks my heart."

He dropped his head in his hands momentarily before he could continue, then he said, "Two weeks ago I had word from her that she has cancer of the throat. I almost went crazy with grief—especially when I didn't even have enough money to call her long distance. We have to pay for calls in advance. But one of the assistant chaplains of this place saw my distress and said, 'Ralph, you may come to my office and use my phone to call your wife. This is an emergency.'

"While I was in his office making the call, the chaplain suddenly burst in the door, turned on me, and yelled, 'Get out of this office. You know this phone is for legal use only. You have no right to use that phone.'"

Ralph's face whitened as he relived that moment, and then he continued. "I was so angry that I was afraid of what I might do to him physically. So I marched right to the warden's office, banged on his door with my fist, and shouted, 'Warden, put me in maximum security. I demand that you put me in maximum security.'

"But," he added, relaxing his clenched fists, "thank goodness he didn't but instead sent me back to my cell to cool off. When I got there, I picked up the book I was reading—your little paperback *What Happens When Women Pray*. I started to read the next chapter—'Forgiven As We

Forgive.' Evelyn, I looked at all the blood on my hands" (trembling, he held them out for me to see what only he could still see), "and I suddenly realized that Jesus said in the Lord's Prayer and then in the next two verses that if I didn't forgive others, God would not forgive me the sins I, as a Christian, had committed either.

> And forgive us our debts, as we forgive our debt-
> ors. . . . For if ye forgive men their trespasses,
> your heavenly Father will also forgive you : but if
> ye forgive not men their trespasses, neither will
> your Father forgive your trespasses (Matt. 6:12,
> 14-15).

Horrified, I knelt down and asked God to forgive my attitude toward that assistant chaplain and then asked Him to give me love for that man. He did, and I went back to his office, knocked softly on his door, and said, 'I just want you to know I have forgiven you and love you.' Evelyn, *that was the turning point in my Christian life!*"

Many letters to and from Ralph and his family, and a follow-up visit have confirmed his changed attitudes and behavior. A Christian—radiantly transformed in that prison!

What About Them?
Surprisingly, I seldom hear from those who have been forgiven. Almost all of the reports are from those who have done the forgiving. Frequently, the ones being forgiven don't even know they have wronged someone or that a grudge was being held against them. Surprisingly, the one who has committed the wrong has often not been injured by attitudes nearly as much as the one who needs to forgive them. The reason Ralph was so changed was not because of the *response* of the official he forgave (he didn't even bother to tell me that). It was because of what happened *to him*.

I find so many people counter this command to forgive with, "What about *them*?" "What if they don't want to be forgiven?" "What if they don't *accept* my forgiveness?" "Why should *I* be the one?"

These are questions that usually pop into my mind too. But they have nothing to do with *our* obligations to obey biblical teachings on forgiveness.

The one who has wronged us has his or her own responsibility to confess that sin before the Lord. But that is not *our* concern. "Avenge not yourselves. . . . 'Vengeance is Mine; *I will repay,*' saith the Lord" (Rom. 12:19).

So frequently I hear, "God is unfair to expect *me* to go to those persons who hurt me. Shouldn't *they*, since they wronged me, come to me?" There are many reasons they don't come to us—an unawareness that they have hurt us, pride, stubbornness, the idea that they have a "right" to harbor wrong attitudes. So we don't wait for them; we take the initiative ourselves.

How we love to play the "I-will-if-you-will" game. But that never produces the *gain* which can be ours if we, by taking the initiative, forgive from the depths of our hearts. Somehow, most of the life-changing results occur in the one doing the forgiving. When we give up, voluntarily *lose* our "right" to harbor an unforgiving spirit, *we* are the recipients of huge *gains*.

Statistics of Evil

Are you aware that each of us has an internal "bookkeeping" system? We have one column in the ledger where we record the good things which happen to us, and another where we keep track of the wrongs leveled against us. Year after year these accumulated statistics tip the balance one way or the other. The side outweighing the other has a strong effect on our whole being. If it is the "bad" side, it can affect us adversely.

I heard of a woman who actually has a little book with a page for each acquaintance. She makes an entry each time they say or do something against her. Then when she comes to a predetermined number, she draws a dark diagonal line across that page—slashing off her list of friends! Statistics of evil.

But forgiving does a strange thing to the forgiver's column of hurts. It wipes clean the evil statistics which have been hoarded in the internal ledgers. In 1 Corinthians 13:5, that great love chapter, we read, *"Love keeps no score of wrongs"* (1 Cor. 13:5, NEB). In other words, as in the Phillips translation, "It does not keep account of evil."

It is so easy to compile, keep adding up, the score of wrongs committed against us. We poke them deep down inside ourselves, layer upon layer, instead of forgiving and being done with them. Doctors tell us we actually can make ourselves ill when we push hurts and resentments deeper and deeper down inside. These attitudes eat away at us *from the inside out*, causing emotional and sometimes physical ills.

Interesting research is taking place on this subject. Leafing through a Western Airlines flight magazine while flying home one night, I took time to read an article by a medical reporter. The bold-type quote caught my eye:

"To the physiologist, general terms such as frustration, anxiety, pressure, worry, job tension, conflict, and anger translate into quite specific events taking place *inside* the body" (*Western World*, March-April, 1979).

Recently, I listened to a speaker who was blaming the church (perhaps rightly) for not forgiving him for a sin he had committed. But, as I watched his revealing facial expressions, I felt that his bitterness at not being forgiven was eating away at him like an internal ulcerated sore. I kept getting the message that if "they" would only shape up in their attitude toward him, he would be just fine. But my heart kept crying out to him, "Oh, dear man, your load could be lifted just by forgiving them for not forgiving you."

We may feel there is a personal *gain* in the satisfaction we derive from exercising our "right" to refuse to give up our angry, negative, accusing, wounded spirit. But in reality just the opposite is true. We are the *losers*. The emotional and physical *gains* come when we take our spiritual eraser and wipe the ledger clean—by forgiving.

I was sitting with the dean of women of a Christian college in her office after completing the "forgive" lesson in a chapel series. A group of freshmen girls knocked excitedly on her door. Jumping up and down and waving her arms like a cheerleader, one of them grinned and exploded, "I'm free, I'm free! I forgave her!"

Although I had no idea what she was talking about, the dean's knowing expression and affirmative nod let me know that a campus problem had just been solved. And a pretty freshman student had been released from the burden she had been carrying. She had erased it—by forgiving.

In my seminars I have seen thousands who were defeated and bitter, instantaneously released from burdens they had carried—sometimes for many years. Released, almost with a shudder, as if something that had become a part of their very being was torn loose.

Or sometimes it is a fresh hurt. A weeping, young mother came to me the minute I said the last word at a recent seminar. "I just have to talk to you," she pleaded.

I drew her back of the stage curtains where we could be alone. "My two preschool children, a boy and a girl, were molested two weeks ago by our nephew who was baby-sitting for us." I enfolded her in my arms as she poured out her story and her tears. "But today I've forgiven him!" As she straightened, she said softly, "It's OK now."

Then I prayed a prayer for healing—physical, but most of all, emotional—for the children. And then prayed that God would completely heal the hurt in this dear mother's heart. She stepped back a little and, still clinging to my hands, smiled, "It's all right now. It's more than forgiven—it's OK." Then, as if she had to convince me even further, she said, "It *really is* OK," and disappeared into the crowd. Eyes still moist, but shining with deep, profound victory. A ledger wiped clean!

So who are the *losers* when we keep compiling, adding up those statistics of evil against others? And how do we become winners? The ones who *gain*, who are victorious, free from the crippling canker that eats away at us, are not the ones we forgave. They may not even have known there was a problem. No, the ones who gain are the *ones who do the forgiving!* The "statistics of evil" column of the internal ledger—which can cause so many emotional mental and physical ills—in our whole being—has been wiped clean!

Sometimes it is easier to "forget" than to "forgive *and* forget." Instead of really wiping it all clean, we feel that just to "forget the whole thing" will take care of it. But it won't. The evil statistic is still inside us—gone only *temporarily* from the conscious mind. Then every time we feel like licking our wounds, accusing that person, or vindicating our hurt again, the ugly statistic comes popping up at our bidding to assist us.

There is one more important erasing that must be done in order to have complete emotional and physical healing. We sometimes forget there is one other person involved—myself. After we have forgiven others and God has forgiven us, we must wipe *us* off the ledger of evil statistics too. Forgive ourselves!

Preventative Medicine

An added dimension to a clean internal ledger is: *Don't let evil statistics accumulate in the first place.*

One of the most strikingly beautiful women I have ever seen is a 60-year-old fellow speaker whom I met at a retreat. After we had prayed through our exercise of forgiving someone, she explained to me, "Evelyn, I honestly could not think of anyone to forgive. You see, for years I have practiced forgiving immediately. Never holding anything against anybody."

Frequently, people try to tell me that, but their faces contradict their words. But the radiant glow on her face and the spring in her step attested to the truth of her statement. Here was a beaming, radiant woman in her 60th year who was living proof of what happens to a face that through the years has not compiled statistics of evil. Preventative medicine! Handsome men and beautiful women!

I've heard it said that we are responsible for our own faces after 40. The lines and sags distribute themselves according to the expressions we have exercised through the years. No matter how perfect the features, facial beauty disappears from the countenance harboring the "right" to be touchy, to hold onto grudges or an accusing spirit. The most beautiful features can never compensate for a mouth pursed with resentment, and with corners drooped in touchiness; eyes narrowed with vindictiveness—surfacing from their statistics of evil column. But the plainest features somehow come alive with a radiance and beauty when they exude, not peevishness, anger and resentment, but love—unconditional love. *Gaining* through *losing* the right to harbor an unforgiving spirit.

Modern medicine is stressing not just healing for existing ills, but preventive measures as well. But the formula has existed for two centuries in the Bible. In all my Bibles I have used since I was 18 years old, I have underlined Ephesians 4:32, "Be ye kind to one another, tenderhearted, forgiving one another." Here was God giving *me* a prescription for preventive medicine through all those years.

Families Reunited

One of the greatest gains I have observed from simply forgiving is the reuniting of families when one member gives up his or her "right" to harbor an unforgiving spirit against another.

A young married woman confided to me that her pas-tor-father had severely wronged her mother by being un-faithful. She bit her lip to keep from crying as she con-fessed, "I'm having a terrible time forgiving him. Pray for me that I will be able to."

Then she handed me her name tag to remind me to pray for her. I did—then and since—that she would be able to forgive—to reunite a bleeding family.

I remember how many years it took me to really forgive my daddy for a wrong I felt he had committed against my mother. I was the *loser* for all those years. I now look back and see how my mother was so much more the *gainer* by her ability to forgive—so much sooner than I.

A daughter-in-law came to me during a local seminar angry, uptight, bitter toward her mother-in-law. "What can I do? She's impossible to get along with," she moaned.

I told her to wait till the next lesson—which just hap-pened to be "Forgive." A couple of weeks later, a com-pletely changed daughter-in-law grinned at me and winked. Peace, tranquility, Christlike maturity communi-cating to me she had found the answer—forgiving her mother-in-law.

While I was leading a prayer seminar in the church that Hansi (author of *The Girl Who Loved the Swastika*) attends in California, a woman came to her and wailed—in German, "I can't stand my mother. She did so many cruel things to me when I was a child. So I came to America. And we get along just fine as long as there is an ocean between us. But I just got a letter that *she* is coming to America!"

"Why don't you come to our prayer seminar tonight?" Hansi suggested. Again the topic was "Forgive." When the alternate rows of people turned around to form prayer groups of four, Hansi found herself in that woman's group. As they each prayed forgiving someone, the woman forgave her mother for all her childhood hurts. As she opened her eyes, she was looking right into Hansi's.

Surprised, she exclaimed, "Oh, *now* my mother can come from Germany!"

At a college, the students shared with each other what had happened after forgiving someone at the seminar the week before. One freshman said, "The courts took me away from my mother four years ago for what she had done to me. After forgiving her, I took the weekend off and went home. Sitting across the kitchen table from her, I said my first words to her in all those years—'Mother, I want you to know I love you.'" Reunited!

In a large southern city, a woman came to me with tears in her eyes and said, "I haven't talked to my mother for 18 years, but last night I forgave her." Then, beaming through her tears, she announced, "And I'm going home for Thanksgiving!"

Then there was the woman in Alaska who knelt, trembling, at my feet as I sat autographing books. Putting her arms around my waist, she lifted her tearstained face and whispered, "I have hated my mother for 24 years. Today I forgave her." Compiled statistics of evil!

"When I was 15 years old, my father committed a crime against my body so severe that he went to prison for it," said a deeply hurt 70-year-old woman. "I became a Christian, but never forgave him and never talked to him so I could share my Jesus with him. Today he is in a Christless eternity, and it's my fault. What can I do to confirm the love I feel for him how that I've forgiven him today?"

"You will never be able to make it right with your dad in a Christless eternity," I explained. "All you can do now is make sure it is all settled between you and God," I explained. How sad to refuse to forgive and to carry a burden like that—for 55 years!

Marriages Too
Not only families, but also marriages are frequently mended by the simple act of forgiving. After my plane

landed in the East for a seminar, the pastor's wife briefed me on their church's prayer chains and groups. "We've had a miracle take place. If so-and-so tells you her story, listen. It's a miracle!"

At lunch I was sitting next to so-and-so who told me, "My husband was fooling around with his secretary and decided to leave the children and me to live in a motel, so he could spend his nights with her. When I helped him pack his bag, I tucked in a Bible, even though he never reads one." (I stopped her and said, "Hold it, Honey. I've been told this story is a miracle, and it surely is. If my husband ever leaves to spend his nights with his secretary, *he can pack his own suitcase!*" But, of course, I knew that really wasn't the miracle.)

"Every day," she continued, "the children and I prayed for our daddy, and every week the prayer chains and groups at church prayed for him. Then one Saturday morning after he had been gone several months, I read in my morning devotions:

> The Lord hath been witness between thee and the wife of thy youth, against whom thou hast dealt treacherously; yet is she thy companion and the wife of thy covenant. And did not He make one? . . . Therefore, take heed to your spirit, and let none deal treacherously against the wife of his youth (Mal. 2:14-15).

Her eyes narrowed with resolve as she continued: "'Hey,' I said to myself, 'I'm the wife of his youth. He doesn't have a right to treat me like this,' And I began to pray, 'Lord, send him to Malachi 2.' *Oh, what a stupid prayer.* 'Dear Lord, send him to Malachi 2.' *What a dumb prayer. He never reads the Bible.*

"But *that very night* my husband came to his senses. Realizing what he had done to his children and me, he started pacing the floor and was contemplating suicide. Then he flung himself on the bed with his head hanging slightly over his partially unpacked suitcase. And there in plain view, out from the midst of the clothes, was—yes, that Bible." (Now you've probably guessed the miracle.)

"He grabbed it and, in desperation, just opened it at random. Yes—to Malachi 2! He read those words, ran home, and begged us to forgive him, which, of course, we so eagerly did." Another family together again.

But on the way back to the plane, the pastor's wife exclaimed, "That story was only half told. That wife was in my prayer group today. While we were forgiving someone, she just stood there, relaxed. She already had forgiven him. But suddenly she became stiff as a board. Then she blurted out her prayer—forgiving *the secretary!*" Wiping the ledger clean!

As a seminar closed in Canada, a lovely woman said to me, "I was to go to my lawyer next Wednesday for the final step in my divorce. But, after forgiving my husband today, I'm going home and tell him I love him instead. You saved a marriage today." No, not I, but *she* saved a marriage that day—by forgiving. Wiping her ledger—full of a long list of evil statistics—clean!

Furthering God's Work on Earth—By Forgiving

We have all seen many examples of the way forgiving furthers God's work here on earth. In Genesis 50:20 we read of Joseph, the young man so deeply wronged by his brothers who sold him into Egyptian slavery. But God meant it for good . . . that many people should be kept alive. What a "right" Joseph had to hate them! But, because he was willing to forgive them, God's chosen nation was preserved.

A missionary on furlough shared a particularly moving experience when she was our guest at our United Prayer Ministries Chrismas party. During Idi Amin's reign of terror, hundreds of refugees fled for their lives to her compound, which was right across the border from Uganda.

She said, "For the most part they were professional people who had lost all their material possessions and many even blood relatives to his plundering, torturing, and brutal murders. I had to go to another mission for 10 days, and was worried about them not having anything to keep their minds off their troubles. So I gave them your *What Happens When Women Pray* to read while I was gone. They were shocked to read what Jesus said about the sins of His followers being forgiven only if they would forgive others.

"When I returned," she continued, "I couldn't believe my eyes. One by one they were kneeling in prayer—*forgiving Idi Amin!*"

After all their losses, who of us wouldn't say they had the "right" to their feelings against Idi Amin? How horrifying were their columns of statistics. But when they were willing to *give up* those rights, their *gains* were almost unbelievable. Transformed refugees!

Their new lives in Christ couldn't be contained. With a new peace and joy, they went out to witness as others watched the incredible example of what Christ really can do in the lives of those who are obedient to Him. Then our guest beamed and said, "In all my life as a missionary, I have never seen such powerful witnessing."

In our own state, we have had the privilege of observing a forgiving spirit on the part of our Christian governor. Right after the Americans had been taken hostage in Iran, some Iranian students reportedly attempted to kidnap the governor of our state. Shortly afterward, we were enjoying hot cider while talking with one of the governor's close friends. "How did he handle it?" I queried.

"He is the most amazing man. His concern was his love for them. No matter what people do to him, he always reaches out to them—in love—forgiving them!" Exuding Christ's love.

A seldom-mentioned teaching of Christ deals with the matter of forgiveness. When we bring our gifts to the altar, if our brother has anything against us, we should leave our gifts and go *first* and be reconciled to him. When the matter is settled, then we should come and give our gifts. We like to omit the reconciling, thinking that somehow enough of the gift-bearing will replace that obligation. (See Matt. 5:23-24.)

Even in our churches, the cause of Christ is often thwarted by the members' refusing to forgive. At a church where I was to speak, the Sunday bulletin had already been printed with my subject listed. But at 11 o'clock Saturday night, God suddenly directed, "Change your topic. Speak on 'Forgiving.'"

At the close of the church service, I did something I had never done before. I asked anyone who had anything against anybody in the church to come to the front and kneel. To my surprise the pastor was the first one. Then another man came and knelt, putting his arm around the pastor. Many others from the congregation met by twos at the front. As he drove me to his home for Sunday dinner, the pastor demanded, "Who told you?"

"Told me what?"

"To change your message to 'Forgive.'"

"God did—last night at 11 o'clock. Why?"

His words tumbled out. "I am on a national committee that voted for something with which I do not agree theologically. Although I told my people that I had spoken and voted against it, one man didn't believe me. He had started a campaign to oust me as pastor. Today some of the members were circulating a petition for my removal. I thought I had completely forgiven this man, but while you were speaking, God showed me I really hadn't. So I came to kneel and forgive him altogether."

Can you guess who the man was who knelt with the pastor? For several years since, I have watched with interest the way Christ has worked in that church—with the same pastor!

Revenge—Forgiveness

A stately black woman, a clinical professor of surgery in a large southern hospital, was addressing us in the Bahamas. I listened carefully as she described the racial hatred and sex discrimination through which she had to claw and crawl to become the first black woman surgeon in the South. Then with a beautiful, radiant smile, she said, "But no revenge is so complete as forgiveness."

Revenge—forgiveness? I pondered that puzzling statement for days. What did she mean? Not revenge by her fabulous success story? Not by showing them that she could do it. How had she *won by forgiving?* She had wiped all the resentment and bitterness out of her heart—in the act of forgiving! She was changed. She was released. She was the beautiful, radiant surgeon—transcending and living victoriously above all their hurtful acts. No statistics of evil left in her to eat away at her from within. Her ultimate victory—forgiving!

Jesus demonstrated this kind of victory on the cross. Triumph over His enemies came not only when He was raised from the dead. Oh, no. It also came *during* the physical torture and spiritual anguish. Victory came as Jesus, while suffering excruciating physical and spiritual agony on the cross, practiced His own admonition to us: *"Pray* for them which despitefully use you, and persecute you" (Matt. 5:44). The complete victory was in His prayer, "Father, *forgive them;* for they know not what they do" (Luke 23:34). Why? Because *they were no longer His enemies.* He was Victor!

I wiped tears as Tim Showen reviewed for me and showed me pictures of what he was going to share at Judson College Chapel before I brought a message on forgiving. And many students also wiped away tears as he told his story:

"Our theme for today is going to be on forgiving as we forgive, and I would like to share with you some Scripture from Colossians 3:13:

> Bearing with one another, and forgiving each other, whoever has a complaint against anyone; just as the Lord forgave you, so also should you (NASB).

It's the first time I've really been able to speak in front of people about this, but about nine months ago I was involved in an auto accident that just changed my entire outlook on life. I was then enrolled in Indiana State, and one day I had spent the whole day with my fiancee—making honeymoon reservations, picking out the tuxedos, and everything. We were two months away from being married.

"And a quarter to 4 that afternoon—from nowhere—a drunk driver hit us head-on. I looked over at Rita, and it didn't take much to tell that she was dead. I was filled with rage and I didn't realize that I was hurt myself. I was in shock and I burst out of the car and ran over to the car that hit us. I was pounding on the car with my fists. I was calling the driver a murderer and inside, inside I was really thinking if I could get in that car I was going to kill this man, and I mean that.

"And all through the months of last summer, I went on with the burden of this hatred in my heart, and I knew it was wrong but I really didn't care. I wanted revenge because he had taken away something that was precious to me, and it really hurt. The strength that I had in the Lord kept me going, but still there was something wrong.

"Then I had to go back to Indiana for the trial of this man who had hit us. I had never seen him since the day of the accident. A friend said, 'I'll be praying for you, for *there is something you have to do*, Tim. You have to forgive this man.'

"I looked at him and said, 'What are you talking about? You want me to forgive this man who took away someone who was more precious than anything to me—just took her away from me?'

"Then he quoted to me, 'Father, forgive them, for they know not what they do.'

"But I'm not Christ. I don't have the strength to say anything like that. I hate this man.

"In court, after waiting and pacing all day, I sat down in

the witness stand and would not look at him. The prosecutor gave me a stack of pictures of both cars. And then there was a short recess.

"In that quiet courtroom I saw the picture of his car and my blood all over it. All of a sudden the Holy Spirit convicted me and shook me and said, 'Tim, look. Look what you've been doing. You wanted to kill this man. And this man was drunk and he had no intention of killing someone.'

"I was really convicted and remembered what Christ went through on the cross—the nails going through His hands and His feet, and the thud as the cross fell down into the ground. And He just said, 'Forgive them. They don't know what they are doing.'

"I glanced over at the man. At the same time, he looked up at me—and I couldn't talk to him. That was not allowed. But in that exchange of glances, I think I was able to communicate: 'I forgive you. Do you forgive me?' And that was really hard to do. But Christ said we have to forgive."

Is there something *you* have to do?

10

Losing My Rights to My Money

When I was a little girl, I divided everybody into two classes: givers and takers. In my mind I didn't see people as short or tall, black or white, fat or thin—only as givers and takers. It was not the giving or receiving of money that was discernible to me at that young age, but much more obvious things. The givers shared what they had while the takers were always trying to get or keep. The takers were the scrooges of the neighborhood, always building their own "empires," reputations, egos. The givers always offered bunches of grapes or carrots from their gardens; but the takers' harsh words or threatening gestures sent little feet scurrying home.

Yet somehow at the end of the summer, the givers never seemed to lack carrots to preserve or grapes for jelly. I sorted out those facts early and filed them away in my little mind for future reference.

Then there was the friendly iceman who always chipped off little extra pieces and conveniently looked away as hot, sweating children clamored aboard his wagon. And there was the grouchy iceman who didn't need to bother to yell his cross warnings to us. We knew who was who!

We had all the cooks pegged as givers and takers too. The mothers of the neighborhood baked homemade bread or buns every Saturday, and we knew which ones never "had enough" in the batch and which ones we could count on for a hot treat smeared with melting butter.

I puzzled over the fact that the takers never got richer than the givers. And the givers never seemed to lack more often than the takers—even through the Great Depression.

But my little preschool mind had also figured out a pattern. The givers not only shared their goodies, they shared themselves. It was the givers who would return the "Hi," who freely gave their smiles.

As I grew older, the categories remained. We knew the ones we could count on to buy whatever we were selling; the ones who would always thank us for working so hard to collect for that "very worthy cause."

Then I made a really big discovery. The takers were usually grumpy and sour; but the givers were pleasant to be around. They were the happy people!

Now I know that those principles I saw lived out in my neighborhood are the same ones we have been given in the Bible.

Seeming-Losses in Scripture

The Bible seems to say such harsh things about our possessions. So opposite to our culture today. It does not commend the accumulation of wealth, but instead the giving up and losing of it.

A professor of New Testament at a seminary who just returned from a sabbatical in Sweden talked with me about our current grasping, materialistic lifestyle. He said, "While away I became more and more overwhelmed with what Jesus had to say about material possessions in Luke 14:33:

> So therefore, no one of you can be My disciple who does not give up all his own possessions" (NASB).

"Evelyn," he continued, "that *give up, forsake,* in the King James Version, literally means *'bid farewell to.'* It is the same word used by Jesus when He sent the multitude away and went alone to pray on the mountain" (see Mark 6:46).

Jesus said these jarring words on the way to the cross. Many of those following Him thought they had latched on to an earthly ruler who would usher in material utopia. But Jesus set their thinking straight. Unless they bid farewell to their possessions, they could not be a disciple of His. A distant follower, perhaps, but not a disciple.

There are many other seemingly harsh words spoken by Jesus about money and possessions: "You cannot serve both God and money" (Matt. 6:24, NIV); "With what difficulty shall they that have riches enter into the kingdom of God!" (Mark 10:23, SCO); "Woe to you who are rich, for you are receiving your comfort in full" (Luke 6:24, NASB). And on the list goes.

Testing

It is not easy to write about the subject of money—especially since God has tested me personally on the theme of every chapter in this book as I've been writing it.

Driving Mrs. Tim LaHaye, author of two best-selling books, from our airport a while ago, I shared this fact. "Is it true with you too, Beverly?" I queried.

Thoughtfully she agreed, "Yes, in everything I write, God tests me also."

While working on this chapter, I have joked with my secretary, Sally, telling her she had better sit on the checkbook as I write. But our slight uneasiness is not without grounds. Sally was there the last time I tried to write about money. She watched as I kept trying to type the story about it in the *"Lord, Change Me!"* manuscript from my penciled notes. I kept ripping the paper out of the typewriter and crumpling it—only to try again—in vain. Although the story was absolutely true, I could not get it typed.

Then the phone started ringing. Three times. The first call was from a woman who had collected all the reservation fees for a large seminar and luncheon at a hotel, while I had signed for the expenses on my American Express card. She said she had some personal debts and had used the seminar money to pay them—assuring me the $1,200 would be forthcoming immediately. (That was three years ago, and to this date I have received a total of $8.) The next call was equally shattering. A seminar chairperson had reversed her agreement with us so that she, not we, would have the profit of the sale of over a thousand books. This profit usually took care of our overhead expenses. The next call was so relatively insignificant I can barely remember the details—except that the losses represented in those three phone calls totaled $2,400—out of my checkbook! More than was there!

Shocked, I got up from the typewriter, put my arms around Sal and let a few tears fall. Then, settling it, I prayed aloud, "O God, it's all Yours. All my money. It's OK!"

The burden lifted instantly. I smiled and said, *"I guess all God wanted was my attitude."* I sat down and immediately typed the illustration. Not that I hadn't given God all I owned before that. No—this was just His testing!

I sat on the edge of the bed last night and said to my husband, "Chris, it really is true that God has tested me on every chapter I've written for this book. I've relived every loss about which I'm writing. Are we *really* ready for me to write about money—or should I take another subject for this chapter?"

He looked up at me and softly replied, "It's okay. We've been without money before." All He wants is our attitude!

Losing through Seeming-Gains

Although the current philosophy seems to emphasize striving for and amassing material wealth, Paul has some frightening words about the outcome of that process:

> But those who want to get rich fall into tempta-
> tion and a snare and many foolish and harmful
> desires which plunge men into ruin and destruc-
> tion. For the love of money is a root of all sorts of
> evil, and some by longing for it have wandered
> away from the faith, and pierced themselves with
> many a pang. But flee from these things, you
> man of God (1 Tim. 6:9-11, NASB).

Paul uses three little terms here that clarify the biblical
position on the dangers of wealth: WANT. LOVE. LONG
FOR. All three result, not from having, but from trying to
get money. Our attitude! Sounds like three terms I might
have used as a child to describe the takers of my neighborhood.

The things that appear to bring gains to us can have just
the opposite effect. Money and material possessions,
God's Word says, actually can bring severe and devastating losses into our lives when they become the ruling force
of our existence.

Greed has created many sad, lonely people. "I haven't
spoken to my brother since our parents died and the in-
heritance was divided up several years ago," shared a
woman at a prayer seminar. "My brother and sisters became very angry with me when the estate was settled. I
kept trying to communicate with them with no response
until seven years ago when I sent my last Christmas card
to my brother. When he didn't answer, I said to myself,
'Phooey to you. If that's the way you want it, OK. I'll
never write again.' Then at yesterday's session I forgave
him, and last night spent many hours tracing his several
moves by long distance telephone calls. When I finally
found him living in another state, I told him I had forgiven
him and loved him."

"Oh, Sis," was his reply. "Since our family broke up, I
have become a Christian, and I have looked and looked for
you but couldn't find you. I've wanted to tell you that I
loved you too."

Typical? Yes. Broken relationships over money at the death of a relative are the most common result of those three little terms. Years of loneliness and lost love come because of bitterness and greed. How easy to sell the love of family, security, and oneness for a few dollars, some old china or furniture.

But even worse, these three little terms can produce a broken relationship with God. Jesus warned about that possibility. "You cannot serve both God and money" (Matt. 6:24, NIV). He did not say, "You cannot *have* money—but you cannot *serve* God and money."

How easy to "go away sorrowing" like the rich young ruler because of *wanting, loving,* and *longing for* material possessions. When Jesus told him that the one thing he lacked was the willingness to sell all that he had and give to the poor, and thereby gain treasure in heaven, his face fell and he went away grieved (see Luke 18:18-27). What could God have done with that young leader? He had it all—authority, wealth, and the vitality of youth. A whole life to give to God. But lost—the joy that might have been his. And ours?

Then Jesus sadly said to His disciples, "How hard it is for those who are wealthy to enter the kingdom of God!" (v. 24, NASB) When Peter reminded Jesus that the disciples had left it all to follow Him, Jesus assured them that all who had done so would receive one hundredfold in this present age and eternal life in the world to come. How much have we missed because of those three little terms— want, love, long for?

Jesus gave us a parable about these terms. "You fool!" said God to the farmer who concentrated on building and filling more and more barns with grain. "This very night your soul is required of you; and now who will own what you have prepared?" (12:20, NASB) Jesus summed up all the words with His stern admonition in Matthew 16:26: "For what is a man profited, if he shall *gain* the whole world, and *lose* his own soul?"

Many people think they were not only born with a silver spoon in their mouth, but that they will leave this earth with a gold one. But neither is true. Paul wrote:

For we have brought nothing into the world, so we cannot take anything out of it either (1 Tim. 6:7, NASB).

In this verse Paul is referring to Job's ancient cry of worship to the Lord. When it was reported to Job that all his material possessions (plus all his children) were gone, he fell to the ground and worshiped, saying:

Naked I came from my mother's womb and naked I shall return there (Job 1:21, NASB).

Whether the possessions of King Tut or those of an ancient peasant were buried with them, or the Cadillac with the owner propped up in it in our day, the soul has been separated from those possessions. And it will never be coming back to get them.

For many years my pastor-husband kept himself reminded of this fact by keeping on his desk a motto from the diary of martyred missionary Jim Elliot: "He is no fool who gives what he cannot keep to gain what he cannot lose."

The Haves and the Have-Nots

Paul, in continuing his teaching about worldly possessions in 1 Timothy 6, divides people and their riches into two categories: those who *want to* get rich (v. 9), and those who are *already* rich (v. 17). There are possible losses for both in their seeming-gains. After giving instructions to those who want to become rich, Paul adds two warnings to those who are already rich:

Instruct those who *are rich* in this present world not to be conceited or to fix their hope on the uncertainty of riches (1 Tim. 6:17, NASB).

First, Paul is saying, "You people with money, *don't be conceited*." Pride is always spelled s-i-n in the Bible. The reason for not being conceited is as old as Moses, who in effect asked the Israelites, "Take a look at the source of your riches." He reminded them that God gave them water and manna in the wilderness. "Otherwise, you may say in your heart, 'My power and the strength of my hands made me this wealth.' But you shall remember the Lord your God, for it is He who is giving you power to make wealth" (Deut. 8:17-18, NASB). No room for conceit there!

Paul's second warning is directed to those who already have riches: *"Don't fix your hope on the uncertainty of riches"* (1 Tim. 6:17, NASB).

I lived through the Great Depression as a little girl and watched the devastating effect on people as the banks went broke. Everything was gone in an instant. My cousin, a bridegroom at the time, was ready to buy all the furniture for his new home, and the bank containing all his savings closed. My father was wiped clean overnight.

Now on the other end of life, I'm living through inflation. Security for retirement? It's like chasing an elusive bubble—always just a little out of reach. Carefully planned insurance and security programs are totally insufficient for those whose earning power has ceased. Missionaries are unable to live on their allotted support funds because of the high rate of inflation in the countries where they are serving. Citizens of other countries have had their currency and savings become instantly worthless as opposing political regimes have taken over the government.

We have no hope in riches. How our seeming-gains can so quickly evaporate—and turn to losses!

Gains from Seeming-Losses

But there can also be gains from seeming-losses. God has recorded in His holy Word the *whys* of His instruction on seeming-losses of material possessions and money. He knew from eternity past that the *givers*, not the *takers*, would be the happy people. So He told us which pursuits, priorities, and principles would produce those qualities of life we all are seeking. Here are just a few of those eternal truths:

Confidence. The Bible gives a tremendous reason why we should be free from the love of (one of those three little terms—*want, love, long for*) money. Why? Because it produces confidence.

> Let your way of life be free from the love of money, being content with what you have; for He Himself has said, "I will never desert you, nor will I ever forsake you," so that we *confidently* say, "The Lord is my Helper, I will not be afraid. What shall man do to me?" (Heb. 13:5-6, NASB)

This is a freedom which cannot be guaranteed by any country's constitution or bill of rights. It is freedom which only we can give ourselves. It produces confidence because of who our Helper is—Jesus Christ. Placing our trust in Him with the assurance that He, unlike uncertain riches, is "the same yesterday and today, *yes* and forever" (v. 8, NASB). One of God's eternal truths!

Contentment. This is one of life's most prized possessions. Paul in another Scripture portion gives us a peek into his secret of being free from another one of those little words—"want." *Being content.* Contentment comes from making do rather than always wanting more wealth. In explaining why his contentment is not dependent on the gifts of the Christians at Philippi, Paul reveals his philosophy of wealth:

> Not that I speak from want; for I have learned to be content in whatever circumstances I am. I know how to get along with humble means, and I also know how to live in prosperity; in any and every circumstance I have learned the secret of being filled and going hungry, both of having abundance and suffering need (Phil. 4:11-12, NASB).

Contentment in the Greek means self-sufficiency. Independent of changing circumstances. Detachment from reverses of fortune. Looking back, I realize how true this has been in my life.

There are two periods in my life which stand out as times of great contentment: during the Great Depression when as a small child I felt the enormity of the decision as to how to "invest" that rare nickel at the candy store; and while following my husband from post to post during his pilot training in World War II, trying to live on $50 a month. I was sometimes a little hungry, but never dissatisfied. Only contented. God's principles really have been a reality in my life.

Just before he gives us those three little terms of which to beware, Paul tells us that if we have food and covering— we should be *content* (see 1 Tim. 6:8). This is not an exhortation, but a statement, a dogmatic assertion of fact that the way to contentment is in *not wanting*. And an eternal fact.

Life. After all the warnings in the Bible about seeking riches, surprisingly we find that it also shows the gains for those who are rich. Paul instructs Timothy to tell these believers the way to have tremendous gain—real life:

> Instruct them [those who are rich] to do good, to
> be rich in good works, to be generous and ready
> to share, storing up for themselves the treasure of
> a good foundation for the future, so that they
> may take hold of that which is life indeed (1 Tim.
> 6:18-19, NASB).

How is this real life available to those who are rich? By being *rich in good works, generous,* and *ready to share!* My husband listened as a pastor lashed out at any Christian who owned a Cadillac—while sitting in front of him were two men who did. But together they were almost supporting a whole mission field.

A doctor's wife in my prayer group startled us with these words: "I'm praying for more money." Then laughing heartily as she saw our shocked expressions, she said, "Oh, not for *me*—so I can give it away!"

Another eternal principle: real life comes, not from having, but from sharing.

Joy. This is a much sought-after quality of life. One of the puzzling precepts shared by Jesus is that it is "more blessed to give than to receive" (Acts 20:35, NASB). Joy comes with giving away; losing—not gaining—money.

I hesitate to write this portion, for as I was reviewing the joys received when I have given, God flashed a Scripture verse across my mind. "Let not thy left hand know what thy right hand doeth" (Matt. 6:3). "Oh, oh," I said half aloud. "How then can I write this chapter?"

But an amazing thread has been running through this whole *Gaining Through Losing* manuscript—*joy.* So, how can I leave out money?

These joys do not come from expected or contrived reactions. No, I'm usually surprised by a spontaneous, unheralded outburst from within. When I was informed that my first book was to be translated into Chinese, the thrill of the potential was exhilarating. But the real joy came when I read that there would probably be little royalty payment. My heart soared at the thought. The *privilege* of being able to give the book was one of the greatest joys I have ever experienced. No twinges of "I wonder how much I'll be losing," or, "It's *my* book; they can't do that to me." No, only complete, engulfing joy!

The same reaction came when I received an inquiry about teaching my prayer material to a large international missions organization. "Lord," I prayed, "give me the *privilege* of teaching them." And as I added, "No money, Lord," a great joy surged through me. Then spontaneously I prayed, "Lord, give me the *joy* of giving them all the books—free." Not negating the verse, "For the worker is worthy of his support" (Matt. 10:10, NASB), but affirming 2 Corinthians 9:7:

> Every man according as he purposeth in his heart, so let him give; not grudgingly, or of necessity; for God loveth a cheerful giver.

Just a secret of the source of joy!

This year I checked with my sister to see if her reaction had been the same as mine when I made a decision about our uncle's will. Our only brother had preceded our uncle in death. Because of the wording in the will, our brother's children were unintentionally left out. Legally, nothing was theirs. But when I made the phone call explaining that it was my wish to divide my share, I was surprised at the surge of engulfing joy that flooded my whole being.

"Oh, Evelyn," said Maxine, "that's exactly how I felt when I decided to share too."

My mother, the greatest giver I've ever known, joined in with her jubilant, "Me too" at sharing her part of that will. Not our loss—but our gain—from sharing! Again, God's principle from eternity past: "It is more blessed to give than to receive" (Acts 20:35, NASB).

But is there joy in giving for those *who have nothing to give?* Yes. To encourage those in Corinth to support the poor in Jerusalem, Paul relates to them the startling example set by the churches of Macedonia in their extreme poverty:

> That in a great ordeal of affliction their abundance of joy and their deep poverty overflowed in the wealth of their liberality. For I testify that according to their ability, and beyond their ability they gave of their own accord, begging us with much entreaty for the favor of participation in the support of the saints (2 Cor. 8:2-4, NASB).

When my mother's oldest sister was ready to go away to school to study to become a teacher, she worked hard to buy the one new dress to take with her. Yet she didn't look on herself as being poor. She and her family always managed on their farm to produce enough food for the winter, livestock to butcher, and chickens to fry.

But from that frugal setting, prompting her little brother to comment to a dinner guest, "Go easy on the butter. Ma wants to sell some," my mother recalls the gaunt, undernourished appearance of a little school friend. One day while waiting for my mother to get ready for school, her friend left her dinner pail in my grandmother's kitchen. Grandma Wyatt peeked inside. Only dry soda crackers. From that day on, her little lunch bucket mysteriously contained a sandwich from their "abundance." Joy? Oh, yes! Just another one of those seeming-paradoxes of Jesus. It truly *is* "more blessed to give than to receive."

No anxiety. One of life's most precious endowments— freedom from worry. In exhorting us not to be anxious, Jesus contradicts the driving motivation of most people today.

> Do not be anxious then, saying, "What shall we eat?" or 'What shall we drink?" or "With what shall we clothe ourselves?" . . . For your heavenly Father knows that you need all these things. But seek first His kingdom and His righteousness; and all these things shall be added to you (Matt. 6:31-33, NASB).

Jesus was speaking of needs, not wants, one of those three little terms of which Paul speaks. It is easy to confuse the two. A friend in the top social stratum of a large southern city told me that she decided to obey those words of Jesus and live on the basis of her needs, not her wants. "It was just like going through drug withdrawal," she confided.

As I was giving this chapter a final reading with my husband, I just finished the preceding paragraph when my phone rang. "You may not remember me, but I saw you in California last week. Evelyn, do you need $2,000?" Stunned, with needs versus wants so fresh on my mind, I stammered that I really didn't *need* $2,000. Then I suggested to her a couple of Christian organizations that desperately did need her money. When I hung up the phone, I felt trembly all over. I wondered if this was another one of God's tests. Had I passed? I realized that if she had said, "Do you want . . . ?" or, "Could you use . . . ?" my response might have been different. But *need?* Then I sighed with considerable relief as I realized that my response had been a spontaneous, truthful one. "No, I don't *need* $2,000." My real attitude surfaced under pressure. Is that all God wants?

Once we get *wants* versus *needs* straightened out, we can turn to the reason for our not being anxious—the Source of our supply. "And *my God* shall supply all your needs according to His riches in glory in Christ Jesus" (Phil. 4:19, NASB). When we set our eyes on the enormity of the wealth of our heavenly Father—who owns the whole universe—we can relax. God's pursuits, priorities, and principles produce that abundant life in Christ.

Your Balance Sheet—Profit or Loss?

When God initiated these principles of profit and loss, for whose profit were they? His own? He, who owns all the land, oil, and other precious resources on earth? Whose balance sheet is it that tips heavily on the "profit" side through these principles? Ours! Paul said, "Not that I seek the gift itself, but I seek for the profit which increases *to your account*" (Phil. 4:17, NASB).

The Bible, in its instructions concerning money and material possessions, says, "All these things shall be added *unto you*" (Matt. 6:33); "For this is *to your* advantage" (2 Cor. 8:10, NASB); "Give, and it will be given to you; good measure, pressed down, shaken together, running over, they will pour into your lap. For whatever measure you deal out to others, it will be dealt *to you* in return" (Luke 6:38, NASB). Filling the profit columns of our balance sheets!

Gamblers for God

It seems that without the willingness to risk losing, there can be no great gains in God's economy. Retired bank president Chester Eggen said to me, "I'm thinking of doing some seminars on the spiritual application of 'There

Is No Gain Without Pain.' As a bank president, I know we must let go of our profits in order that we can earn more profits."

A pastor-friend whose wife is in real estate commented, "I know I could make money in investing, but I'm too chicken!" And God's Word affirms this truth in the spiritual sense:

> He who sows sparingly shall also reap sparingly;
> and he who sows bountifully shall also reap
> bountifully (2 Cor. 9:6, NASB).

Our nonprofit United Prayer Ministries organization decided to test that principle. From its inception, the love offerings had never quite paid the travel, publicity, and mailing expenses. So, after much prayer and with our treasury still in the red, we voted to launch a giving program—free books, tapes, and leaders' guides to missionaries and prisoners. To our surprise, at the end of that fiscal year, we had enough money left over to buy a typewriter and a desk— and the trend has never reversed itself. It works!

Jesus' Words

God set in motion all the laws of cause and effect long before they were recorded in sacred Scripture for us. He wasn't surprised when He saw the principles working in His human creatures on Planet Earth. He knew they were true all along.

Then Jesus, who in the beginning was with God and was God, came down to Planet Earth bringing with Him the words of the Father for us. And when He was ready to go back to His Father in heaven, He prayed in His high priestly prayer: "Father, I have given unto them the words which Thou gavest Me" (John 17:8).

Jesus, in order to bring words to us, temporarily gave up His godly prerogative as Possessor of the entire wealth of the universe, to be born in the poverty of a cattle stall:

> For you know the grace of our Lord Jesus Christ,

that though He was rich, yet for your sake He became poor, that you through His poverty might become rich (2 Cor. 8:9, NASB).

He was willing to bid farewell to all His possessions so that we might become rich. Not as measured by the world's gold standard, but in God's infallible economy.

Now these words that God sent down for us about givers and takers were not just commands God decided arbitrarily to impose on His creatures. No, He knew from eternity past what would bring real gains. So He gave us the rules, not as a harsh taskmaster, but as an all-loving Father graciously explaining to His own how to get the end results of joy and happiness for which we all are longing. Thus, instead of demanding a poverty mindset through seemingly difficult scriptural principles, He actually opened the lid of a vast treasure chest—revealing to our shocked eyes the secrets of the ages. Gaining through losing!

"What shall it profit a man if he GAIN the whole world and LOSE his own soul?"
—Jesus Christ

11

Losing My Right to Be an Unfit Christian

"I've never seen a happy jogger," a friend confided to me. I agreed, admitting that I frequently slow down the car to get a better look at a sweating, sometimes struggling, figure with the grimacing face. Exercising!

Because much of man's physical labor has been replaced by push buttons and elevators in our mechanical age, the need for exercising the body's muscles through various programs has become imperative. So wherever we look we see the puffing, panting beginner or the sleek, invincible expert valiantly striving to build up and tone down.

Contrived, organized and meticulously timed exercise programs—these are good. With today's emphasis on preventive medicine—precautionary measures—exercise is part of a lifestyle that helps keep us well. In addition to physical benefits, the experts tell us that exercise produces a whole array of good results—a pleasant mental state, an exhilarating lifestyle, an antidote to depression, the ability to respond to stress and pain and, if not years to one's life, certainly, life to one's years!

But there is another kind of exercise program—a spiritual one—which builds up our inner man. I find myself wondering why so much importance is placed on being in shape physically and so little on being spiritually fit. Also, since physical exercise is so exhilarating, producing such profound feelings of well-being, why are we so skeptical and apprehensive about spiritual exercise? Why do we try so hard to avoid it?

God's Exercise Program

Before the foundation of the world, God knew we would need spiritual as well as physical exercise. So He placed in the Bible His spiritual exercise program. Surprisingly, I have discovered that, as does physical exercise, it produces the same exhilarating lifestyle, pleasant mental state, an antidote to depression, the ability to respond to stress and pain, and adds life to one's years!

But what *is* spiritual exercise? Don't be surprised if you don't know. In the Book of Hebrews we are told that we have *all* forgotten God's method of exercising His children, as set forth in Proverbs 3:11-12, so the writer reminds us:

"My son, despise not thou the chastening of the Lord . . . for whom the Lord loveth He chasteneth . . . afterward it yieldeth the peaceable fruit of righteousness unto them which are EXERCISED thereby" (Heb. 12:5-11, Caps are mine).

Exercised by what? By an often misunderstood biblical word—*chastisement*.

Accepting this teaching is often difficult because of our negative concept of the chastisement—assuming it to mean "punishment." This causes us to think that all the hard things which come to us are God's form of retribution for our wrongdoing. But the accurate definition of that word is "discipline, training." How different! The purpose is just the opposite—not punishing, but perfecting. God assuring us that the things which come into our lives and the things which He sends will be used by Him to *exercise* us—to make us fit for the tasks and trials of life.

William E. Vine, in his *Expository Dictionary of New Testament Words* (Revell, p. 183), says that "the word *chastening* primarily denotes training children: suggesting the broad idea of education by (a) correcting with words, reproving, admonishing, or (b) by chastening by the infliction of evils and calamities; suggesting the *Christian discipline that regulates character.*" Back in Ecclesiastes 3:10 is recorded, "I have seen the travail, which God hath given to the sons of men to be *exercised* in it"—God's exercise program.

Strangely, the writer of the Book of Hebrews calls this forgotten process an *exhortation*, which means "encouragement or strengthening consolation." I should be encouraged or consoled by the infliction of evils and calamities? Adults, not just children? Strange reasoning by today's standards.

But trials are not to be resented nor do they represent unjust punishment from God. They are just a part of our moral training, designed for us, and used by our heavenly Father to further the education of His children.

At 18 years of age, I underlined in my Bible, in red, Deuteronomy 8:5, "Thou shalt also consider in thine heart, that, as a man chasteneth his son, so the Lord thy God chasteneth thee." But then I understood little of God's future spiritual exercise program for me.

Losing My Right to Be Free from God's Exercise Program

Do I have a choice?

I do have the right to choose if I will engage in a bodily exercise program. But as a Christian, I have *lost the right* to choose whether or not I will be spiritually exercised.

> For whom the Lord loveth He chasteneth, and scourgeth every son whom He receiveth. If you endure chastening, God dealeth with you as with sons; for what son is he whom the father chasteneth not? But if you be without chastisement, whereof all are partakers, then are you bastards,

and not sons (Heb. 12:6-8).

If I am never exercised by God, then I am not truly a child of God. But when I am exercised by Him, I know I am His child. As such, I have lost my right to be a flabby, unfit, unexercised Christian. The choice is not mine.

And even more astonishing is the fact that it is the one whom God loves, that He chastens, disciplines, and trains. It was through our Judy, afflicted with spina bifida, that God's exercise plan for me was unfolded. (See *"Lord, Change Me!"* Victor, pp. 29-31.)

When the doctor told me that Judy (at that time just five months old) would not live, I didn't have any problem knowing that I was a real Christian—and one whom God loved. But God chastening the one He loves—like that? In our sorrow we sometimes become angry and blame someone. Frequently it is God. I have never blamed God, but I did become very angry with the pastor of my home church. After my mother told him about Judy, his immediate response was, "God must love Harold and Evelyn a lot to give them all that sorrow."

Those words stung and burned deeper and deeper as I knelt by my bed far into the night. Judy's temperature had soared to 105° in a couple of hours that morning. Later in the day, the doctor had said not even to stop at home after leaving his office, but to take her right to the hospital. Then came the awful void of my first night without her. For hours battling with God on my knees by my bed— becoming more and more angry with the man who had so abruptly said those shocking words.

"Sorrow!" How could *he* understand? Had he been there during the awful labor that produced the baby paralyzed from the waist down? Had he heard the head nurse say, "I thought you would like to know, you had the hardest kind of labor this hospital records"? Had he been there when my kind Christian doctor walked alongside my cart as I was being wheeled back to my room, holding my hand, trying to keep me from hurting too much as he explained, "Everything is not good with your baby. In fact, it looks pretty bad. Spina bifida, some paralysis. Tests tomorrow."·

How could that pastor have known the ache in my heart, as a new mother, when everybody had gone home that first night, and the sympathetic head nurse, Miss Payne (how I smiled afterward at the appropriateness of that name for the labor room of that hospital), sat by my bed stroking my hair with her tender hands, and applying the cool wet cloth to my burning, tear-filled eyes and throbbing forehead. How could he know *that* sorrow?

But our pastor had said, "*All* that sorrow." In my anger, I relived the sorrow of my stillborn's birth. Of laboring— in vain. Two whole days in the final stage of labor, trying to deliver the baby I had known for 10 days was already dead. And the two miscarriages. My anger grew.

But deep down I knew that what he said was in accordance with Scripture. And I had never doubted God's Word. I never had been angry with the God of those Scriptures. So numbly, still on my knees, I reached for my Bible on the nightstand to read Hebrews 12 once again for myself—"For whom the Lord loveth He chasteneth" (v. 6).

Yes, it was all there. I had really known it all along. What that pastor had said was true. But in my crushing sorrow, there was a vague feeling of something being unfair—or at least beyond my understanding. The King James Version had used the word *chastisement,* and I bent lower and lower under it. I didn't doubt that God loved me, but *this* to express and prove His love? The thought swirled foggily through my befuddled, bowed head.

Suffering chastisement, the writer to the Hebrews said in essence, was a sign not of God's displeasure, but of His *love.* I knew that love was one of God's attributes. He *is* love, and His actions cannot be inconsistent with who He is. The Bible clearly stated that *He* was the one doing the chastening.

So I learned about losing my right to be free from God's exercise program—because I knew I was one of those whom God—the God who *is* love—loved. *Losing my right to be a flabby Christian!*

For My Profit—Gaining Through Losing

But God didn't leave me wounded and broken under this puzzling proof of His love. This was the point at which He gently nudged me to read on.

I recall the words *exercised by it* just standing there, hazily, as if the printer should have used more ink—completely beyond my grasp. But the three words that seemed to be in the printer's bold type for me were in verse 10:

> But He [chastens] FOR OUR PROFIT, that we
> might be partakers of His holiness (Heb. 12:10,
> Caps are mine).

When the frenzy of a current physical exercise program diminishes, there is sometimes the realization that all that was produced was not necessarily for the exerciser's profit—runner's shin splints; blisters; orthopedic problems with knees, back, and feet; tennis elbow, or even a rare exerciser's heart attack. But not in God's program. His is always *for our profit*.

What do I gain from spiritual exercise? The same results that are gained from a good physical exercise program! I'm amazed at the parallels I find. Identical!

George Blanda, who retired from the National Football League at the age of 48, indicated in his recent book, *Over Forty: Feeling Great and Looking Good* (with Mickey Herskowitz, S and S Enterprises), that the more the body is exercised, the better is its ability to respond to sudden stress and other work in general. It is also true that the more I am spiritually exercised, the more strength I have to cope with the sudden stresses brought about by adverse circumstances or attacks from the enemy. The more I have been disciplined, the more efficiently I am able to respond to day-by-day hard work for God.

While reading James Fixx' best-seller *The Complete Book of Running*, I kept smiling to myself as I saw the astounding parallels between the glowing results from physical exercise and the results of being spiritually exercised by God. "We don't guarantee to add years to your life," he writes, quoting Robert Glover, physical fitness director of the West Side YMCA, New York City, "but life to your years" (*Book of Running*, Random House, p. 9).

Are a zest for life, exhilarated feelings, sparkling eyes, a glow and radiance produced only by physical exercise? No. These are also a part of the abundant life that Jesus promised. And He has really produced this exciting lifestyle in me; but, surprisingly, it has come through a difficult spiritual exercise program.

At a Christian Booksellers' convention I sat looking at Joni, that quadriplegic author of two best-selling books, star of the movie of her own life, and founder of an organization to help others who are handicapped, and saw all of these qualities exuding from her. Because she had been swimming, diving, or hiking? Oh, no. While immobile in her wheelchair! What produced her glow, her radiance, and exuberance? Physical exercise? No—spiritual exercise! What God had produced in her *since* that devastating diving accident which left her paralyzed from the shoulders down.

"There's nothing quite like the feeling you get from knowing you are in good physical condition. You wake up alert and singing in the morning and really ready to go," writes Mr. Fixx, quoting a runner from Massachusetts (*Book of Running*, p. 9). Sounds familiar! That's just the way I feel after I've been spiritually firmed and built up by God's exercise program.

Again, writing about what people say physical exercise produces, Mr. Fixx says, "Such factors as willpower, ability to apply effort during extreme fatigue, and the acceptance of pain—have a radiating power that subtly influences one's life" (*Book of Running*, p. 14). Exactly what I experience as a result of being spiritually chastened and exercised. When we were discussing this, my former next-door neighbor, Betty, said emphatically, "It works. I watched it for almost 15 years."

James Fixx also noted, "Running (being exercised) is a powerful antidote to anxiety, depression, and other unpleasant mental states . . . an ideal antidepressant" (*Book of Running*, pp. 15-16). Yes, I too can assuredly face life without a worry or a hassle, being anxious for nothing. It is because of God's chastening program that I can know absolutely that God has prepared me for everything He will allow or send my way. I will never have to worry about overexercised spiritual muscles, knees, or feet. There will never be a spiritual heart attack from overexertion. All fear and apprehension about the future is gone. I will always be spiritually prepared!

At the time of Judy's final crisis, while there on my knees, God unfolded His spiritual exercise plan to me. I could hear Him saying so clearly, "*For your profit*, Evelyn." Then He said, "If you're going to be a pastor's wife, you will have to understand some of these things." Then I read the rest of Hebrews 12:10:

"But He for our profit, that we might be PARTAKERS OF HIS HOLINESS" (Caps are mine).

Mr. Fixx quoted a young editor who was working on *The New Yorker:* "A good run sort of makes you feel holy" (*Book of Running*, p. 15). The Bible says that a good exercising by God *does* make you holy. God chastens and exercises us spiritually that we might be *partakers of His holiness*. The process that makes us holy as He, the God of the universe, is holy. In fact, in the comparison of physical and spiritual exercise programs, Paul goes so far as to say, "Bodily exercise profiteth *little*, but godliness is profitable unto *all* things" (1 Tim. 4:8).

When?

So many people have asked me *when* they could expect these great results from being chastened and exercised by

God. The very next verse in Hebrews 12 gives the answer:

Now no chastening for the present seemeth to be
joyous, but grievous, nevertheless AFTERWARD
it yieldeth the peaceable fruit of righteousness
unto them which are exercised thereby (v. 11,
Caps are mine).

But when is afterward?

In heaven? "It will be worth it all, when we see Jesus,"
serenely, assuredly, sang our close friend, Faye, with her
teeth and jaw still wired in place after the accident. It was
her first solo since an oncoming car, in an attempt to pass
another in a blinding snowstorm, hit her car head-on. Her
husband, her only child, and her mother were killed.

Were the words she was singing so confidently in her
sorrow true? Absolutely. How thrilling to think of heaven,
where all of God's reasons for and results of His exercise
program will be unrolled like a scroll before our eyes. Not
our sometimes-manufactured "whys" to satisfy our de-
mands for answers or the inquisitiveness of others, but the
real, the fabulous profits from His exercise program (see
2 Cor. 4:16-18).

But does *afterward* refer only to heaven? I remember the
day God showed me that there is an "afterward" here on
earth too. It was on a critical day of a very deep family
trial. While I was studying for my Bible study in 1 Peter, I
came to chapter 5, verse 10:

But the God of all grace, who hath called us unto
His eternal glory by Christ Jesus, AFTER THAT
YOU HAVE SUFFERED A WHILE, make you
perfect, establish, strengthen, and settle you
(Caps are mine).

I cried out in prayer, "O God, *when* is 'after awhile'?"

I recorded that cry to God in the margin of my Bible and
dated it. Then almost four weeks later when I was to teach
that verse again, I resignedly wrote in the margin, "When
is God's after a while?" Then I answered my own question, "Not yet!"

It wasn't till a whole year later that I scrawled in large bold letters on that page, "NOW is God's after a while. Great joy again! I'm finally settled. To God be the glory!" Through the years, God has given me the privilege of experiencing countless "after a while" periods—after the exercising is done and the results can be measured—right here on earth.

Now while I was going through that time of chastening, the experience certainly didn't seem joyous. But a careful study of that verse in 1 Peter helped me understand what was happening *during* my trial. I discovered four things God was doing for me: (1) *Making me perfect.* Restoring a part which was lacking, repairing a weakness, and mending me. (2) *Establishing me.* Making me as firm as granite. Instead of collapsing under the weight of the trial, I was coming through it with spiritual muscles like tempered steel. (3) *Strengthening me.* Toning up my flabby inner man. (4) *Settling me.* Laying my foundation solidly on bedrock. Anchored on The Rock—Jesus. This produced in me the peaceable fruit of righteousness.

Chatting with me on an airplane, a woman returning from a trip to Japan remarked, "I had a $100 steak dinner there. The meat was so tender I cut it with my butter knife. The cattle had been kept so immobile that they could not develop any tough muscles. Then they were massaged by hand to further soften their flesh—until they could no longer even stand up."

That, I thought, *may make for a good steak dinner, but it won't produce great people.* When I am being matured by God, He doesn't only soothe and caress me, He gives me an exercise program that spiritually strengthens me.

During

But does spiritual exercise mean I can never be happy *during* my trials? No. Paul told Timothy, "Exercise thyself rather unto godliness. For bodily exercise profiteth little, but godliness is profitable unto all things, *having promise of* the life that now is, and of that which is to come" (1 Tim. 4:7-8).

All joggers are not unhappy. Though they strain for more air in their lungs, they may be enjoying their exercise immensely. Tom, a young seminary student, came trotting in for breakfast like a young horse with his tail to the wind, having had a good run; his body glistening with sweat, his skin aglow. He explained to me the "high" he had reached that morning while jogging his 10 miles. At that point, his effort had turned into sheer joy.

Just as a jogger experiences the exhilaration of strain during exercise, the invigoration of blood racing through his veins, the euphoric "high" during a good run, can't we expect a "high" *while* being spiritually exercised? Perhaps others see only our sweating, our struggling, and our occasionally grimacing faces. But, if they slow down and take a closer look shouldn't they be able to see an inner exuberance as we spiritually strain against the wind? Yes, they should, because the challenge of being stretched, the rush of spiritual adrenaline for the struggle, can produce the same glow that results from physical exercise—not just afterward, but during the trial.

Bitter or Better

My husband and I missed the morning business session of a convention as we sat spellbound at the breakfast table listening to our surgeon-friend explain his views on "bitter or better" from Hebrews 12. His face glowed as he recalled the time when Chris had put him on a plane in Chicago and afterward when he arrived at home he had found his wife comatose, after suffering a severe stroke. Then he told us about his daughter, the wife of a young doctor, who, during pregnancy had become ill with polio. He told us how they struggled to save her and the child, and of the decision he made that the moment had come to try to save only the baby's life. Then of the death of both, recalling the casket with his daughter holding the tiny infant in her arms.

In the past we had so admired the exuberance and excitement of his full, well-rounded life—Sunday School superintendent of the largest church in our conference, highly esteemed surgeon, tennis champion. But the glow that morning was not the result of having just finished an exhilarating tennis match, or even the flush of one of his national tennis tournament victories. No, that glow was from God's exercise program—spiritual exercise.

"It all depends on how you respond to trials," he explained, eagerly leaning toward us, radiant and serene. "Bitter or better. And the only difference is one letter—*I* changed to *E*. And the *E* stands for 'Emmanuel—*God with us*'. The secret is when the *I* of me changes to the *E* of Emmanuel—Jesus!" Our Coach!

Keep Your Eyes on the Coach

And the secret to victory during the exhausting training and the rugged athletic event is to keep your eyes on the coach!

Eric Heiden, winner of five Olympic gold medals for speedskating in the 1980 Winter Olympics, commented during a television interview that the crucial thing he did to win was to take his eyes off his human competition and *put them on his coach.*

We can look unto Jesus, who not only is our Coach, but also our Example:

> And let us run with patience the race that is set before us, looking unto Jesus, the Author and Finisher of our faith; who for the joy that was set before Him, endured the cross . . . lest you be wearied and faint in your minds" (Heb. 12:1-3).

Our Example shows us how He endured during His trials. The reviling, the nails, and the excruciating death were certainly not joyous to Jesus. But still He endured, looking forward to the joy of His after a while—sitting down at the right hand of the throne of God.

Eric Heiden must have remembered his day-after-day, year-after-year disciplining as President Carter, welcoming him and other 1980 Winter Olympic athletes to a White House luncheon, said:

> "It's hard for [some people] to appreciate what it means to get up before dawn, year after year, when others are still asleep . . . to endure pain and exhaustion and disappointment. . . . To go through all that pain and sacrifice is indeed a great achievement" (*Minneapolis Tribune*, February 26, 1980, p. 1A).

Eric had tangible evidence of his gain from that sacrificial training—five shining, first-place gold medals.

And so it is with us. Our great Coach—God—puts us through a tough training program—because He always goes for the gold!

And what do we profit? The seeming-*losses* turn into the same great *gains* that are only to be attained by the most grueling, sacrificial spiritual training possible. But the greatest gain of all is that we are fit for the Master's use!

Spiritual exercise. Some never let the Coach get started with the training. Others don't stay with it long enough to ever experience that possible high. Some just get bitter instead of better. And then there are those glowing, radiating participants—spiritually exercised!

Are *you* fit for the Master's use?

12

Losing My Right to Be Free from Suffering

When you received Christ as your Saviour and Lord, were you informed of the rights you could expect to gain? They were myriad—the right to find life, abundant life; the right to have the power of Christ rest upon you; to have God fill all the voids left by human losses; the right to life after death in an eternity with Jesus; the right to expect God to come in proportion to your every need; the right to expect to bear fruit; the right to expect to have good mental health. These are but a partial list of the rights that were promised to you, that you could expect to gain when you took Christ as Lord of your life.

On the other hand, did someone also tell you that if you became a Christian, all the problems of your life would disappear? So you accepted Him, and felt you had the right to expect the bumps of life to smooth out. Now the gains you did have the right to expect when you became a Christian were fabulous—but the right to be free from suffering and difficulties was not one of them. In fact, according to Scripture, that seems to be one of the rights you lost the moment you became Christ's.

In the Epistle of Philippians, Paul wrote these startling words:

For unto you it is given in the behalf of Christ, *not only to believe* on Him, *but also to suffer* for His sake (Phil. 1:29).

Both? Doesn't it say, "If you believe, your suffering will be removed?" *Expect* to suffer?

To young Timothy, Paul reiterated the same thought by telling him "*all* that will live godly in Christ Jesus *shall* suffer persecution" (2 Tim. 3:12). Not even "may," but *expect* to?

Don't be surprised? That's exactly what Peter said: "Think it not *strange* concerning the fiery trial" (1 Peter 4:12). In this passage the word *strange* is best translated "surprising." Are you surprised? I have underlined these verses in all of my Bibles since I was 18 years old. Yet when I put them all together for this book, their impact surprised me.

There seems to be a progression of reactions to suffering that comes as we mature in Christ. *Reject* it . . . just *accept* it . . . then actually *expect* it.

By now are you questioning the wisdom of ever "signing up" for such a religion? But let's look more closely.

Gaining T-H-R-O-U-G-H Suffering

The sufferings recorded in the Bible seem so frequently to be related to gaining. There is a little word—an important preposition that shows relationship—that is the key. *T h r o u g h.*

A speaker introducing Joyce Landorf at a convention said, "Every time I see Joyce, she has just come through a crisis." I suddenly saw what a compliment that was, and when I had an occasion to introduce her, I explained to the audience: "He did not say she was *in* a crisis, but had just come *through* a crisis—making her the successful author/singer/speaker that she is—giving her insight and answers for the people whom she is addressing.

But we cannot come *through* one without being *in* one.

The Bible (and history) is full of examples of God's great ones who suffered in various ways—persecution, personal losses, physical suffering. But their suffering was not an end in itself, but just a *means to an end*. The victories, triumphs, and gains which came through these sufferings are astonishing. Gains by losing? Yes, *losing the right to be free from suffering*.

In this book we have looked at the suffering and difficulties of some of God's heroes and heroines. The spiritual giants in the Bible were not free from hardships. The list is endless. What terror Joseph must have experienced when he was sold into slavery by his brothers—but selected to be God's person to preserve His chosen people from famine. And Moses, snatched from his family in Pharaoh's slaughter of the male children, then living in obscurity for 40 years on the backside of the desert—being prepared to lead God's chosen people to their promised homeland. And Paul—through beatings, stonings, shipwrecks, hunger, cold, nakedness, imprisonment, and pain—reaching his world, and all following generations, for Christ. Then Peter suffering amidst persecution along with other first-generation Christians—equipped to encourage and buoy up "God's elect"—then—and now. And the beloved Apostle John, suffering isolation in his exile on the Isle of Patmos—but receiving from God the revelation of things to come—for all generations until Christ returns. Then, of course, the most important on the list of God's chosen ones, His own Son—who suffered so that He might bring fallen man to God. Gaining, through losing the right to be free from suffering!

Fellowship of His Suffering

For even hereunto were ye called, because Christ also suffered for us, leaving us an example, that ye should follow His steps (1 Peter 2:21).

These startling words were written by Peter. We are called to be like Christ—but even in His suffering?

Paul, in explaining his philosophy of *gaining through*

losing all for Christ (Phil. 3:7-10), concludes with three *so thats* resulting from this process: "That I may (1) know Him, and (2) the power of His resurrection, and (3) the fellowship of His sufferings." But how common it is for us to want to know only the first two—just two-thirds of what Christianity is all about—Him and power. But the remaining third—the fellowship of His sufferings—we so frequently leave off our list of wants.

The chairman of the government arm of our thousand-member, city-wide telephone prayer chain just this morning said to me, "I took Philippians 3:10 as my life verse when I was a teenager. I meant it with all my heart, and was very sincere about it. And I've consciously worked at living according to it ever since. But as the years have passed, I've discovered I was only concentrating on the first part—that I may know Him and the power of His resurrection."

She shook her head and continued, "But it finally dawned on me that that was only part of the verse. The rest was 'and the fellowship of His sufferings'. . . ." It was so easy for me, also, to take just two-thirds of what Paul said—or even what the whole Bible says.

This is not to say that suffering is *never* removed. However, it is when I get past the idea that the *only* gain possible from suffering is to have it removed, that I mature into Christlikeness—what He was able to be in His sufferings. Not enjoying the suffering, but with Christ, willingly enduring all that is God's will.

But what did Christ suffer while here on earth? Only the cross? No. Sometimes we think that the crucifixion was Christ's only suffering. Then we can feel secure in the remoteness of the possibility of our being martyred for Him. But Jesus' whole ministry was laced with suffering—many different kinds—while He was doing His Father's will.

Peter, who probably did not witness Christ's death on the cross, was yet able to say, "I who am also . . . *a witness of the sufferings of Christ*" (1 Peter 5:1). Therefore, Christ must have suffered in other ways and at other times. But how? Right after entering into His ministry, Jesus suffered alone under the temptation of Satan for 40 days. But from that time on, Peter was there. He saw the agony Jesus suffered when His former peer group tried to push Him off the cliff at Nazareth. And Peter saw the deep hurt in Christ's face when so many who had wanted to make Him king, turned and followed Him no more. He watched as Jesus wept over Jerusalem with a broken heart. And Peter, a member of Jesus' inner circle of three, was so near to the agony of Gethsemane as Jesus wrestled in prayer with the Father. But it was *only* Peter who saw the anguish in his Lord's eyes as He turned and looked on him, after he forsook and denied Him, just as Jesus was facing His greatest physical and spiritual suffering—crucifixion.

Is the tenderness that exudes from Peter's first letter, his suffering epistle, the result of his having experienced these sufferings with Jesus? Is that what sends me fleeing to that book when I am hurting? Is this the reason God so graciously led me to teach that book in my neighborhood Bible study when the deepest grief of our pastoring years occurred? Is this why I get the feeling that this is the book that understands me?

Early one Sunday morning in the midst of tunneling through 1 Peter for the writing of this chapter, I asked God not to let me just write. But I begged Him to make this chapter *real* to me. Then I slipped down to the living room and, with my heart growing heavier and heavier, once again read through Paul's sufferings in the Book of Acts and 2 Corinthians. Then I sat in silence thinking through all of Jesus' sufferings. Overwhelmed, I prayed, "O God, I am not *worthy* to write this chapter!" Tears were straining to get out of my eyes. I wept. "I am not *worthy* to suffer— *even* to suffer!"

Rejoice
I went back to reading 1 Peter 4:12-13: "Beloved, think it not strange concerning the fiery trial which is to try you,

as though some strange thing happened unto you, but *rejoice."*

"O God," with tears still persisting, I cried out, "how can I rejoice when my heart is breaking?"

Then God gave me the answer from those verses.

"Rejoice because you are *sharing Christ's suffering."* I have a part in the suffering that broke His heart—and mine? I have that privilege? "Yes, it is Jesus—whom you love so much—whose sufferings you are sharing!" said God.

And there was more than just the *reason* for the joy. It actually said to rejoice *in proportion* to our sharing in the sufferings of Christ. "To the degree that you share the sufferings of Christ, keep on rejoicing" (v. 13, NASB). The more *I lose my right to have suffering removed,* the more I *gain* the ultimate privilege possible for any human being: not only being like Christ—but actually sharing His sufferings!

Rejoice—There's Glory

While all the personal sufferings of my life seemed to be marching in shadowy review through my mind, God kept dealing with me. He said next, There is a *so that* to being partakers of Christ's sufferings: *"That, when His glory shall be revealed, you may be glad also with exceeding joy"* (v. 13).

Again my mind slipped back to the man, Peter. How uniquely qualified he was to write about future glory. I have often tried in vain to grasp the magnitude of the glory of the transfiguration. But Peter was a witness as Moses and Elijah "appeared in glory" and talked with Jesus—whose face was shining like the sun and whose raiment was radiating and glistening. When Peter awoke from his sleep, he "saw Jesus' glory" (Luke 9:30-32).

And through eyes still red with weeping after having forsaken and denied his Lord, Peter was the first apostle to see Jesus in His resurrected, glorified body that first Easter. The awe of that glory must have left him prostrate and trembling at Jesus' feet (See 1 Cor. 15:5 and Luke 24:34). Then between the resurrection and ascension, Peter's eyes were opened as Jesus explained the Old Testament prophets' predictions about Christ's sufferings and the glory which would follow (See 1 Peter 1:10-11). So Peter scattered throughout his writings the astounding association between suffering and glory—for me. And my tearfilled eyes, too, beheld Christ's glory!

How different was Peter's understanding from the time when his newfound Messiah had said the strange-sounding words so early in His ministry: "Blessed are ye, when men shall revile you, and persecute you, and shall say all manner of evil against you falsely, for My sake. Rejoice, and be exceeding glad; for great is your reward in heaven" (Matt. 5:11-12). Peter must have thought, "Master, wouldn't it make more sense to say that we should rejoice as our trials are removed?" It would have been natural for him to have questioned Jesus' logic very early in their relationship.

Future Glory

Peter also used this same word *rejoice* in the first chapter of his first letter to explain that sufferings, although necessary, are only temporary—completely transcended by that which is to come. Rejoice because trials have a purpose— to prove the genuineness of our faith which is much more precious than gold—which also must be tried with fire. And then rejoice because *beyond the trials,* at the appearing of Jesus, there will be *praise and honor and glory!*

We can endure, and actually rejoice while enduring, if there is something great enough to look forward to. And that something is a Person—my Jesus. I have not seen either but, believing, I love, and rejoice with great joy too deep for words, transfigured beyond earthly bliss—my Jesus! (See 1 Peter 1:6-8.)

Paul summed it up writing:
    And if children, then heirs; heirs of God, and

> joint-heirs with Christ; if so be that we *suffer with*
> *Him, that we may be also glorified together*. For I
> reckon that the sufferings of this present time are
> not worthy to be compared with the glory which
> shall be revealed in us (Rom. 8:17-18).

Christ's pathway to glory is also our pathway to glory.

Glory Now Too?

That Sunday morning as I continued to meditate on His
Word, God kept adding more understanding about that
glory. This verse I found hard to comprehend: "If you be
reproached for the name of Christ, happy are you; for the
spirit of glory and of God *resteth upon you*" (1 Peter 4:14).
The spirit of glory glowing and radiating God's presence—
on me? The glory of Christ that Peter remembered from
the Mount of Transfiguration? Or the glory John said they
had beheld in Jesus? (John 1:14) Or the glory Jesus had
with the Father before the world was? (John 17:5) Or perhaps the visible brightness of the Shekinah glory as mentioned in the Old Testament, the luminous glowing of the
presence of God among His people?

On me? That possibility seemed absolutely untenable,
impossible. The best I could do was to look back to those
whom I had remembered actually radiating during and
after deep suffering.

While I was Corrie ten Boom's hostess in St. Paul for a
week, I saw that glow on her face as she said to me,
"Every day while I was in Holland during World War II, I
prayed, 'Dear Father, don't send me to the concentration
camp. Don't send me to the concentration camp!' But,
Evelyn, He sent me to the concentration camp! But I now
know why."

Her reason took me by surprise: "*So I could learn to suffer*.
Evelyn, 60 percent of the Christians on earth are suffering
active persecution today. And God has sent me to 63
countries to teach the Christians how to suffer. And Evelyn, God has said to me—it is coming to America. That's

why I'm here." The radiance on her face transcended all the Nazi horror of World War II.

Glorified by Me?

Then God unfolded to me a second reason for present rejoicing during trials. That one I couldn't handle. "But *on your part* He is glorified" (1 Peter 4:14). Then Peter adds, "Yet if any man suffer as a Christian, let him not be ashamed, but let him *glorify God on this behalf*" (v. 16). I, by my attitudes and reactions during suffering not only have His glory resting on me, but can actually glorify *God?*

Then a scene from 10 years ago flashed through my mind. The ache of having decided I was not worthy to serve Christ publicly because of a deep family crisis again engulfed me. But then I remembered my hostess showed me what her husband's mother had written in her Bible at what was to have been my last neighborhood Bible study:

The follower of Christ does not hang his head in shame as the difficulties of life come upon him. He trusts God; and, by his poise and grace in the midst of difficult circumstances, declares to all the world that God is able to deliver, yes, *to glorify Himself* in that which has come to pass.

Then the memory of another Bible filled my thoughts. In it is the first recorded prayer for me—written after I found Christ at nine years of age. My mother bought me that first Bible, and in it wrote the prayer for her daughter:

Mother's Prayer
In life's great journey,
As you travel through,
May GOD BE GLORIFIED
In *all* you do.

Each year I pray a birthday prayer for myself for the coming year. On my last birthday, I prayed, "God, You be glorified in me this year. I want only You to get the glory all this year, not me. All the glory—not just 'You be glorified most and me a little less.' " What an exciting prospect!

What a fantastic gain for me—the God of the universe glorified in *me*! And yet—what an overwhelming thought. Then I hesitated and questioned. Was I being brazen, egotistical, too pushy? Who did I think I was? "In me"— an ordinary, everyday human being—the glory of the God of the universe? The Creator—and I only the creature? Was this a scriptural prayer? Yes it was. First Peter 4:14: "On your part He is glorified"!

As I write, this year is now 11 months old. Has it happened? God has certainly not removed all the suffering from this year, but it has been a year of unprecedented joy. Not that I had expected that prayer to produce joy. But God gave it while I consciously, one by one, gave all the things which could have brought *me* glory—to God— only for *His* glory.

But there is a warning here. All these examples of the connection between suffering and glory indicate that we are to rejoice *only* if we do not deserve the suffering. Christ's sufferings all occurred while He was doing good, and when no guile was found in His mouth (1 Peter 2:22). We rejoice when we suffer *wrongfully*—when innocent like Christ.

God's Will?

All the old wounds of my Bible study class in 1 Peter opened up when I read verse 19 of chapter 4. It had been the capstone then, and became once again for me now— God's will. "Wherefore let them that suffer according to the will of God commit the keeping of their souls to Him in well-doing, as unto a faithful Creator." When? When I am in God's will.

This is God's plan. But it is much more than submitting to an inevitable destiny. It is being able, when in His will, to entrust myself completely to Him. In my prayer seminars, I teach how to pray in God's will. But before I ask people to entrust their souls to Him—in joy or sorrow, victory or defeat, healing or suffering—I point out that they must know *who God is*. He loves us so much that He has dedicated and consecrated Himself to work everything out for *our* good. He chastens for *our* profit. He intends every *loss* to be that through which we can *gain*. *The One who takes all our losses and turns them into gains.*

God is the faithful and powerful Creator of the universe. He has power over all creation—and all suffering. Enough power to do anything He chooses! To transcend suffering—to give grace to endure it, or comfort through it, or to remove it—the decision is His. We entrust it all to God and leave the results to Him.

To be sure, the results are not all the same. But they are always for our eventual gain. Sometimes it is the shock that a prisoner named Ralph experienced after giving his most precious possession, his family, to God. The next morning, Ralph learned that his daughter had been struck by a car and was not expected to live. Through much prayer and a series of miracles, he soon was on his way to her. In the midst of that horrible crisis, he found himself thanking and praising God—what better hands could his daughter be in?

Then there were the results God gave to Doris. Last Sunday I telephoned Dr. Doris Johnson, president of the Senate of the Bahamas, United Nations representative, author of their constitution's preamble guaranteeing religious freedom for her nation.

"How are you, Doris? I've been hearing some great things about you!"

"Oh, Evelyn, you will never believe how the Lord has worked this all out!" she exclaimed. "The mortgage on my house, the pain, all the burdens—gone—since I turned them all over to Him!"

What did she mean? Two years ago at a convention in the Bahamas, she came to me and said she wanted to bring her prayer partner to my room to pray. For almost three hours we sat in a tight circle, knees touching, her prayer partner and I praying intermittently as Doris rehearsed her problems. With her doctorate degree in educational administration, Doris had had a fine-paying job. Her present Senate position held lots of prestige, but not all that much money. Her husband had died. She couldn't keep up with the mortgage payments and was losing her home. She had a pain in her shoulders and neck that no doctor, nor a well-known faith healer, had been able to help. Should she give it all up and go back to making more money?

I finally said, "Doris, can *you* pray now?"

"What should I pray?"

I explained that she should *release it all to God.*

"What do you mean *release?*"

"It's the word *commit* in 1 Peter 4:19. When we suffer undeservedly, we are to turn ourselves over to God. It is the same word Christ used on the cross when He was suffering while absolutely innocent. Jesus, our example, who all through His life entrusted Himself to His Father's will. Even at the time of His supreme suffering, the crucifixion, He committed His soul to His Father. Doris, just give it all to God."

I slipped down on my knees and she dropped her head onto my shoulder. For 15 minutes, with deep emotion, one by one she gave each facet of her life to God—for His will. The next morning at the convention she delivered a beautiful, almost state-of-the-union address.

"That was terrific! How are you?" I bubbled.

"Oh, Evelyn, it's all gone—the pain, the burdens. I'm just great."

On the phone she brought me up-to-date through the two years of God's working out every single thing after she gave it all to Him.

"And," she exclaimed, "the last great thing that happened to me was in October. I was invited to Buckingham Palace and knighted by Queen Elizabeth—with the Dame Commander of the Most Distinguished Order of the British Empire!

"And as the Queen was pinning the star over my heart," she continued, "its hook fell to the floor. While all the attendants and guards stood frozen at attention, the Queen stooped down at my feet and picked it up. All I could think of was: 'AT THE NAME OF JESUS EVERY KNEE SHALL BOW'!"

Immediately I thought, *If we suffer, we shall also reign with Him* (2 Tim. 2:12). The final glory Peter mentions is *the crown of glory* (Cf. 1 Peter 5:4). A crown of exaltation—the victor's crown.

Reigning with Jesus of whom, *through* His crown of thorns, it could be written, "And a crown was given unto Him; and He went forth conquering, and to conquer" (Rev. 6:2). And, because I too have LOST my right to be free from suffering, I have GAINED the greatest of all gains: I will reign with Jesus!

But, until that time, while we are still here on earth, God is in the business of turning all our LOSSES—physical suffering, being forsaken, aloneness, bereavement, forfeited money, and relinquished rights—into GAINS. Maturing us, refining us, strengthening us, preparing us, enriching us—if we let Him.

Are you *gaining* through your losses—with God?

Epilogue

Perhaps you have never experienced God's turning your losses into gains. First, you must be His child. How can you become a member of His family? Realize that "all have sinned and come short of the glory of God" (Rom. 3:23). But God has provided a way for you to come to Him. "For God so loved the world that He gave His only begotten Son, that whosoever believes in Him should not perish, but have everlasting life" (John 3:16). To become His child, you must receive Christ as your Saviour. "As many as received Him, to them gave He power to become the sons of God" (John 1:12).

If you desire this personal relationship with God, pray:

"God, I confess that I have sinned and thus am separated from You. Jesus, I believe that You are God's only provision for my sins, having paid for them by dying on the cross. I receive You, Jesus, into my life as my Saviour and my Lord. Thank You for making me one of Your own."

Pray this prayer sincerely and start a new life with God. And, with Him in control, you will be eligible for God's intended plan for you—His taking your losses and bringing you great gains through them.

And for all of God's children, the secret of this life is in loving Him above all else, deeply desiring His will, and faithfully obeying all of His instructions. As you search for His leading in His Word and listen to Him in communing prayer daily, He is faithful and will reward you.

Write me (4265 Brigadoon Drive, St. Paul, MN 55122) and let our prayer chain pray for you.

Love in Christ,
Evelyn